University of St Andrews Travel Writers' Society

Founded in December 2001, the Travel Writers' Society was established to encourage the art and practise of travel writing within the university student community; to facilitate the accruement of the nuts and bolts of an "author's toolkit" through workshops and lectures; and, to provide outlets for the publication of student travel writing.

Quo Vadis? has been compiled with these aims in mind and is an attempt to showcase the best work of our members and peers. The Society owes a debt of gratitude to each of the contributors whose work you see published within these pages for submitting their articles, stories, journals, correspondence and poetry so freely.

We believe that this publication offers not only an exhilarating journey to the far corners of the globe, but also an opportunity to learn about student life on the hoof.

D0334689

University of St Andrews Travel Writers' Society

Quo Vadis?

An Anthology of Student Travel Writing:
Twenty-Eight Accounts from Six Continents

General Editor - Dawn Slaughter
Senior Copy Editors - Elizabeth Kalfsbeek, Rachel Kondo, Tara Quinn
Information Technology Editor - Rupert Spiers
Design & Layout Editor – David McHutchon
Treasurer – Matthew Craw

Contents

INTRODUCTION: QUO VADIS?
Tara Quinn

The journey towards the completion of this Anthology has been marked by copious amounts of 'grunt work' and guided by the glow of 'final rewards'. This prospect has inspired the Editorial Team from its initial over-ambitious meetings in the Union's Reading Room, to caffeine-charged evenings at Castle Tavern; from a little cottage in Dinnet, Aberdeenshire, back to the Reading Room and finally to a computer lab in North Haugh.

'We need a name for the book,' said President David as we finished an afternoon stroll through Dinnet. 'Let's think of one before we reach the end of this road.' We considered this idly, as the stop sign loomed ahead, and spewed forth with some real winners, including 'Beyond West Sands' and 'Gullible's Travels'- a *real* favourite with the group.

Finally, miraculously, the name appeared barely before the book itself had taken material form. *Quo Vadis?* or "whither goest thou?" begs the question that haunts us all as students and travellers. Where *are* we going? With your submissions of journal entries, articles, and poetry you have tried to show us. Whether your path took you to tiny villages in Uganda or Ghana, a stroll down the Champs-Elysee, a school in India, a hike through Corfu or just around the bend in our beloved St Andrews, the thoughts and memories of this Anthology have demonstrated a lively curiosity and infectious spirit of adventure.

But putting together this book has consisted of much more. Since January, we have gone from a vague idea, to nuts and bolts, to thrilling reality. In a few months there have been endless highs and lows with fears of a submissions deficit, growing into panic over lacking funds and everything else falling in between. And yet, this idea somehow took shape and grew, swelling almost of its own accord, until it was suddenly a matter of mass editing sessions and pondering layout options. We suddenly found ourselves here, at the end of our road.

The editorial team has consisted of an eclectic group of students, as varied as the Anthology itself, with members hailing everywhere from Northern Scotland to Northern Canada, from distant Hawaii to not-so-distant Kirkcaldy, all bright-eyed with dedication, many on their way to new adventures at the end of the year.

The writers featured in this book have inspired us with their words and stories and we hope that you also find yourself both inspired and enchanted by their tales. Ultimately, we are all travellers making our way to the next job or degree or far away place. *Quo Vadis?* is the name we have granted that spirit as we all explore and question and experience on our journey down the road.

ACKNOWLEDGEMENTS
David McHutchon – President, Travel Writers' Society

The first credit for the publication of this book is due to the Committee of the Travel Writers' Society who were willing to devote considerable efforts, in the initial stages, to planning and preparing the Society for the project. On an individual level, our Secretary and the eventual General Editor, Dawn Slaughter; our Treasurer, Matthew Craw; and our Events Officer, Caroline Watkinson, all willingly laboured behind the scenes to complete the requisite groundwork.

The Editorial Team is also tremendously grateful to the contributors for freely donating their work to a project that for certain periods seemed unlikely to succeed. Each of them brings a unique flavour to *Quo Vadis?* and it is my hope that several are able to turn their evident talent for travel writing into a profitable sidelines or even careers.

On a personal note, I wish to thank the dedicated team of student editors who sacrificed many countless hours to convert this dream into a reality. To be able to produce this book in the space of two such defiantly short months has required an effort of Herculean proportions, which must surely stand out as a unique achievement for a University Society and an individual triumph for each of them.

The greatest debt, however, is due to the University of St Andrews and the Student's Association for their financial assistance in this the first and most difficult year.

Thank you all.

SAFARI STORY
Paula Stiles

"Sois calme, or they will charge," the guide whispered in French. About forty feet away, a large group of African Elephants splashed and played in the waterhole. The baby was cute, but it was the very large bull, flapping his ears and watching us with suspicion, which held our attention. Fortunately, we were downwind, but the wind could always change. Coming early in the morning to the park had turned out to be a wise decision. By the time other visitors arrived, the elephants had finished bathing and moved off into the brush.

Despite having lived for over a year in Cameroon since my arrival in December 1991, I was just as excited as my visiting parents to go and see Waza National Park in the Extreme North Province. The park had been established not far north of Maroua, an Arabian Nights city of cool trees lining hot boulevards and low, whitewashed houses hidden inside wooded compounds. In other parts of Cameroon, most large mammals had been hunted either to extinction or permanent hiding deep in the bush. Even the preserves in the southern rainforest were being devastated by unchecked logging. A bush meat dinner in the Center Province fetched a luxury price on restaurant menus - three times as much as the equivalent in chicken, and over thirty times as much as a kilo of beef.

I had seen many birds and insects, some rodents, and the occasional cobra or mamba near my home in the East Province, but no large animals. Waza contains part of the great savannah band that extends from West Africa through Cameroon and Central African Republic to Kenya. Animals still migrate throughout the year across this band. Waza is the only park in Cameroon that is well maintained. Despite sporadic poaching, one can see all sorts of large mammals there: elephants, lions, giraffes, wildebeest, numerous species of antelopes and birds. February and March are the best times to see it, not just because the heat of late dry season forces the animals to come to the watering holes, but because the dirt tracks through the park are impassable during the rainy season.

The taxi driver who drove us up to the park from Maroua was typical of his fellow Cameroonian colleagues - young and opportunistic yet friendly and helpful. The park guide assigned to us at the gate turned out to be both honest and a veteran tracker who loved the animals he helped protect. We got his attention when we crammed ourselves into the back seat of the taxi and insisted that he sit up front with the driver. We assumed that our guide should have the best view in the car so that he could find the animals more quickly. After seeing the elephants at the watering hole, the rarity of our logic became clear when we met a group of white tourists in a Land Rover. Their guide, whom they had inexplicably stuck in the very back, watched our car longingly as our guide gave the driver an animated account of where the herd could be found. My parents later clinched the goodwill of both the driver and the guide when they shared our lunch with them. After that, the guide spent two hours scouring the nearby area for lions to show us. We finally had to ask him to give up. The lions had obviously retired somewhere until dusk and we needed to get back to Maroua. Despite our disappointment, we had seen many different animals and birds already. It didn't seem right to allow the guide and the driver to endanger themselves by wandering about in the bush trying to rouse a sleepy pride of lions for our benefit. Someday, though, I intend to go back and see lions - albeit from the safety of a very large truck.

I was sick that day, and even sicker the next three days. It had taken me three days and a thousand dusty kilometres by bush taxi and train to travel north from my post to meet my parents at the airport in Garoua (a hundred kilometres south of Maroua). Still, I have never regretted visiting Waza. I love zoos. But after seeing a mother giraffe gallop, steady and straight as an ocean liner, at full speed across the track in front of our car to herd her baby away from us in Waza, I have never since been able to look at a caged giraffe with equanimity. Even in the best zoos, there is no room for a giraffe to run.

Our instructed vagrancy, which has hardly time to linger by the hedgerows, but runs away early to the tropics, and is at home with palms and banyans- which nourished on books of travel, and stretches the theatre of the imagination to the Zambesi.
George Eliot, The Mill on the Floss. [ed.]

WHITE ISLAND
Victoria Quinn

My father and I pulled up in a new red Holden, already looking disreputable. He was wearing a narrow-brimmed blue denim hat at least two sizes too small for him, and I was wearing unfortunate trousers. The launch was deserted, clean and elegant. I was left squatting on our bags, peering out to sea, whilst my father clambered onto and around the launch. He was purring and clucking in satisfaction.

The pier rocked gently with the mud-brown tide. It was utilitarian rather than glamorous, and I was already dreading the ladder. In my mind's eye, I could see myself descending into the cool water in a graceful arc whilst the men laughed and bonded. I've never been good with ladders: my hands and feet forget they belong to me.

Two men in jeans and gaudy jumpers emerged from the fish-packing shed on the scrubby, grubby shore. They were all seamed face and oiled hair. Ignoring me, they went to peer suspiciously at my father. He grinned up at them and waved. They stared pointedly at the smudged footprints he had left all over the white transom and his smile faded.

"G'day," one of them said. It was, simultaneously, an introduction and an interrogation.

"Hello," he replied. "Lovely boat. How many knots does she do?"

"Are you on the trip, then?" asked the other.

"Yes. Colin Perrior. That's my daughter, Victoria, with the bags." Their eyes swivelled round to me and I managed a faint, embarrassed wave.

"Hi." The eyes swivelled back, unblinking.

"She coming too?"

"Yes." They both glanced at each other and the silence held for a long moment.

"Better get you on board then." With a confidence I was far from feeling, I scampered up and down that wretched ladder helping them load our bags. I even leapt lightly onto the deck, swinging myself through the rigging to a ripple of applause from the sea, as it slapped the sides of the boat. "Tide's changed," I said, stating the blindingly obvious. No reply. Then, "I'll go and settle us in then, shall I?"

They had sorted out the pecking order by the time I returned. My father always was good at that. They were having a comfortable grouse about how late the others were. 'The others' were three journalists who would be covering the trip for their magazine. It turned out that this was the first voyage since the boat had been wrecked on a well-known, and mapped, reef two years previously. I sucked on a cold beer and listened to the men talk knots whilst the gulls cried overhead. Truth be told, I was only half-listening, as I was calculating how far I could swim if I had to.

The sun sank below the horizon and a voice came out of the dusk. "Hey, can somebody give us a hand? We've got a lot of kit up here." The journalists had arrived with a trailer full of stubbies, tinnies and tackle. They were plump, hearty men who looked like they talked a good story but did most of their fishing third-hand. By the time they were all on board, we had missed the tide and dinner was fairly subdued. To do them credit though, at least they didn't treat me like I was the Missing Link.

We spluttered out late across a calm, dark sea. My father was glued to the technicolour fishfinder in the cabin, eagerly pouncing on every passing blip; the journalists were swapping whisky and tall tales in a pool of light by the stern; the engineer and the skipper were doing whatever engineers and skippers do, and I was alone with the cold wind and water. I knew then that, provided nobody snored, it would be alright. Well, they all did, but it was alright anyway.

The next day was beige and unlovely. We were rolling badly and I spent much of the morning staring down at my feet, which were braced against the side of the boat. Under my soles, the sea, and under the sea, some soles, I suppose. Eventually, I tired of this and joined the huddle in the cabin. We talked of fish we had caught, fish we had lost, and fish that had got away without any help from us. We took turns staring at the fishfinder and getting excited over nothing. We did stop a couple of times in likely-looking places, jiggling lures seductively in a desperate attempt to attract snapper, but all we caught was coral.

"You'll have some sport at the island," we were promised. "That's where the fish live, see." The engineer was right, which, to be frank, surprised me a little. No snapper mind you, but lots of barracuta fighting to take the hook. They were muscular, predatory fish with mad eyes and scales like silver bars. Riddled with worms, the skipper told us, but great bait.

An unofficial competition developed, never stated but fully understood, between us and the journalists. Much to our satisfaction, we were winning and on their tackle. There had been some confusion over the booking, which had meant that we had thought the skipper was providing the tackle and he hadn't. If it hadn't been for Bob, one of the extremely generous, charming and talented writers who had joined us, it would have been an acrimonious trip.

Our next stop was a small, deserted island even further out. We moored on the lea side and I started jigging with feathered lures whilst the others cracked open some tins. I caught some sweeties; small fish with the deep, smooth curve of a perch. They came up the irridescent blue of a butterfly's wing, but soon faded to a sober charcoal grey. The engineer told me that the Maoris prized them as good eaters, so I dropped them proudly in the freezer box. They looked rather pathetic in that icy vastness. As the sun dipped below the horizon the cliffs took on the rich, strange colours of winter peaches and the fish stopped biting, so I reeled in, packed away and went in to supper.

We hoovered up scrambled eggs on toast which we were soon to find were good because they were all the engineer knew how to cook and so he had had lots of practice. Even the skipper started to thaw and tossed the odd word in my general direction. After supper, he hung a powerful lamp over the stern. Strange luminous fish passed through the pool of light and the moon sat fat on the water. Then they came. Squid. Arrowing up from the depths to leap towards us. They were coral pink, delicate fawn, speckled with gold and rust and they clung to the hooks that we lowered over the side like frantic lovers at an airport. In the bucket however, they just looked tawdry and inkstained. I got quite excited until I realised that everyone else was assuming the fish would eat them; not us. I went to bed at that point.

My father and I shared a small cabin and we were - and are - both big people. He snored, I tossed, and the condensation dripped off the ceiling onto my nose. Grabbing my sleeping bag I crawled on deck. It was a magical night: still, moonlit and rippling with birdsong from the island. I drifted off to sleep with a smile and a sigh, and woke with the sun on my face. It was bitterly cold and I was stiff as the proverbial plank, but the sky was the translucent blue-green of a robin's egg and I could smell bacon frying. God was in his heaven. All was right with the world.

The next leg of the journey went on forever. The sea stayed calm and the fish stayed away. Oh, we tried everything, trolling hefty, feathered lures for tuna and marlin; hanging onion sacks of raw meat and chopped baitfish over the side to attract shark; sending tua-tua and squid flapping down into the depths. Not a nibble. We saw lots, of course. Rolling pods of dolphins, the flap and splatter of a kahawai feeding frenzy complete with gannets, the occasional sharp fin breaking the surface and then sliding out of sight, but none of them came near. Then, on the horizon, we saw a plume of white smoke.

"White Island," said Bob. His face broke into a smile of plump satisfaction. "Luck should change here, Clare. Got out this way once before. Caught a beaut hapuka - 340-pounds. See, off the west side the bottom just drops away - down to about a kilometre. The east side's all broken up. Good for snapper and terakihi. Only trouble is the water's full of those bloody orange buggers. You know, the little ones with the big mouths? Pull one of them up and you think you've got a ray on the line because the water resistance is unreal. When it eventually gets to the surface it's all mouth and trousers and about six inches long." He spat expertly over the side. "Christ! A turtle!" Even the engineer came up to see that.

My father hugged me. "Good so far?"

"The best." We stood there for about half an hour watching the volcano. It stuck out from the sea like one of my Uncle Dave's tombstone teeth. "What do you know about White Island?"

"Just the obvious, really. I think I remember someone saying that they used to mine for the sulphur there until the last eruption, but that's about it."

"I'm going to ask the captain if we'll be able to land. It looks amazing." I ducked under his arm and wobbled into the cabin. The captain only grunted when I spoke to him, but it sounded like an encouraging grunt so I went to get our binoculars from the cabin.

As we got closer, I was stunned. Half the crater wall had been blown away, leaving a high-walled corral with no gate. The sides were striped with arsenic, mercury, sulphur and iron, and steam shot in jets from fissures in the rock. It all looked very temporary. The basin was carpeted with rubble and boulders that all appeared to have been dusted with pollen. Suddenly, Peter, one of the other journalists, gave a shout.

"There it is mate! There's the old station!" He whooped and clapped hands with Bob in what was supposed to have been a high five, but which failed to make the grade. Clamped to the small beach were a thin line of broken palings and a ramshackle tower made from corrugated iron, now pink with rust. Not much had survived. The captain got us in as close as he dared and then dropped anchor. The sound of the rattling chain seemed like sacrilege.

"Anybody still want to land? Only I got to get the dinghy ready." We all could and did hear the blue streak of curses as he disappeared down the starboard side, calculating the number of trips. Well, I think we lasted about fifteen minutes once we got to shore. The wind had been blowing off the sea before, protecting us from a choking smell of rotten eggs lightly tinged with brassica. I was the first to start heaving, but the others followed soon after. We couldn't sit down to recover either, as the ground was vibrating hotly beneath us. The white flag of surrender was waved and we set off back to the boat in double-quick time.

After lunch (scrambled eggs, naturally), we upped anchor and moved around to the western side for some serious fishing. I don't know if you've been deep-sea fishing before, but for those of you who haven't, you drop a lead weight the size of a baby's head overboard, attached to over a kilometre of line and a succession of baited hooks. You then jiggle the rod to see if you have actually hit the bottom, and wait for a knock. If you think you have had a bite, or if your line has been down for more than fifteen minutes, you wind in. You need to wind in at a fast, steady pace just in case you have hooked something without knowing it. Either way, it weighs a ton and takes ages to bring up. By the time you can see the weight, you really don't care anymore about the fish, you just want your arms to stop hurting.

Enough whinging. The fishing was magnificent. It nearly killed me, but it was really something special. I caught a blue-nose cod, a 40-pound hapuka ("Look guys, she's caught a minnow! That's just a baby, sweetheart. Better throw it back, eh?"), two kahawai and four barracuta that snaffled my bait as I was reeling in. Daddy did even better. And the journalists? They got lots and lots of those "little orange bastards". Perriors 2 - Journalists 0.

The east side filled the bins with snapper and terakihi as promised. Not particularly big, but fat as the butter in which we fried them. When we eventually stopped hauling them in, I flipped the lid on the freezer and peered in to gloat. The hapuka, mottled brown and frog-faced, peering back with a hangdog expression; the blue-nose, a discreet chocolate colour except for its turquoise lips; the whiplash silver of barracuta and yellow-finned terakihi; kahawai in their uniform khaki, and snapper decked out in coral sequins for the lobster quadrille.

"Victoria? You want a drink?" came a voice from within the cabin.

"Scotch, please." I pulled the lid back on and went inside.

The drink had to do me until lunch the next day. My shoulders and arms had seized up completely. I collapsed onto the bed at about seven o'clock, fully-dressed, smelling of fish and with a fur-lined mouth. The next morning I sat and watched the men trolling as we turned for home. It had been one hell of a trip, but right then, I would have given it all for a hot bath.

"A lazy man travels around the sun just as fast as a busy man."
R .T .Wombat

"Being in a ship is being in a jail, with the chance of being drowned."
Samuel Johnson
from Boswell, Life of Johnson, 1791

"A journey of a thousand miles starts in front of your feet."
Lao-tzu

JERKING MY MEMORY
Sarah Curnow

Random. I think that would be the appropriate adjective, especially here in St Andrews. Random, and very memorable. On being offered beef jerky again recently, the memories came flooding back: memories of an amusing, chaotic and rather odd evening spent as part of my Australian travels.

We could have stopped at the next town, but dodging the *roos* was becoming a little hazardous; and frankly another four hours cruising along the same outback roads did not seem appealing. I say 'outback' it was hardly Western Australia, or even Western Queensland. After several days of driving, however, I did foolishly imagine we would be somewhere near Uluru, more commonly known as Ayer's Rock. So it was in Morven that we stopped, the choice of motel being quite limited: in we went anyway.

We didn't actually trip over the electric cable lying everywhere and the surrounding caravans were probably only half-derelict. Not quite the type of location approved by *Wish You Were Here?*, but we were just thankful for a town and signs of life.

To be brutally honest, there weren't any signs of life. Well, not many, anyway. But at least on this seemingly endless stretch of road, of whose straightness even the Romans would have been proud, we had finally happened upon a 'town'. A middle-aged woman greeted us. Actually, she was probably younger than that, although her face was weather-beaten and the ageing effect of the intense sun had clearly taken its toll. "We've just one room left," she told us. They had had an influx of guests. We couldn't quite imagine who the clientele would be, until she added that they were road workmen, for whom it was a little too far to commute each day. Yes, we'd take the room, thank-you-very-much. Not too many options available to us really, and with no sign of *The Ritz* further down the road, it wasn't too strenuous a decision.

There were only three beds between the four of us, cosy. The woman brought us a *swag*: a sleeping bag and camping mat all in one. Very Aussie. And very dirty. Perhaps my sister would share my bed instead, although the sheets were really not much cleaner. But we were learning to count our blessings. The toilet was badly stained and I don't think any of us even contemplated having a shower, but at least I couldn't see too many spiders. The other insects certainly looked well established and were probably family pets. We thought it best not to look too closely. At least we had a bed for the night; well, almost a bed.

We drifted through the bar area to get some tucker. A tall, wiry man standing at the bar seemed to be in charge, although we later discovered he was only a long-term guest who had obviously made himself quite at home. He made road-trains for a living: model road-trains, out of beer cans. Oh, and *dunnies*. We could commission one if we so desired. We'd think about it. He proceeded to offer us the beef jerky and in trying our best to be polite, we accepted. Awful. No, we didn't want anything else to eat, thank you. It had quite put us off eating there. Donk sat quietly in the corner. Being toothless, his conversation was quite limited. Maybe he wasn't quite Donk, but he could have easily been an extra in *Crocodile Dundee*. We were feeling quite out of place with our shorts, fair skin, cameras and English accents, though ironically it had only reached twenty-five degrees that day. Even Dad felt rather English in that setting.

When we met Hopper we were certainly ready for some light relief. The lady called for Chantelle to come. Her daughter duly arrived, a girl of about thirteen, who then went to fetch Hopper. I wondered if Chantelle had ever seen a hairbrush and I couldn't imagine where she would go to school. Maybe she hadn't and didn't. Just then, the joey jumped out of the sack. His mum had been run over by a truck on the main road outside and the work-men had rescued her. They kept her in a sack in the bay area, although I don't suppose the Environmental Health people passed through very often. I'd seen other marsupials at close quarters, but at this time of night, in this strange town, it was rather different. Then, pounding into the dimly lit room came a dog. At that moment, the cockatoo was let out of its cage to join in the general frenzy. The cockatoo chased the blue-heeler. The blue-heeler tried to pick up the joey. The joey just seemed to take it all in its' stride.

The next morning, when we had closed the car doors and finally set off for another day of travelling, we left with a sense of bemusement rather than anything else, I suppose. So as I said: random and very memorable. Although I'll perhaps refuse the beef jerky next time, I'll certainly call in again when passing through.

RYOKAN VISIT IN KYOTO
Elizabeth Kalfsbeek

Imagine after a tiresome day of sightseeing how appealing it might be to go out to dinner in your pyjamas. Japanese pyjamas, that is. An that's exactly what you can expect while staying at Yachiyo, a traditional Japanese inn in Kyoto.

At the inn, or ryokan as it is called, expect to immediately "check" your shoes before even entering the door. Along with a claim token, as you would for a coat at a restaurant or dance hall, you receive a pair of slippers for use around the ryokan. They come in two sizes, too large or too small. Though the brown, worn plastic slippers would never make it into *Vogue*, you nevertheless can't help embracing the concept of not wearing shoes indoors, unlike in most Western buildings.

Shortly after check-in, be prepared to be ushered to your room by a Japanese woman clad in very traditional dress and exotic hair. As you are busy surveying the room, and notice with amusement the separate toilet slippers to be worn in the bathroom, you turn around to discover the convoy has brought you a cold coffee/tea concoction to enjoy whilst unpacking.

Upon taking a sniff of the drink and deciding you wouldn't even serve it to your in-laws, you suddenly become overwhelmed by the charming atmosphere. Go ahead, pull up a seat which provides a back rest as you sit next to the serving table just a few inches off the floor. Whilst revelling in being welcomed into the culture, you decide the cold mystery drink isn't so bad after all. In fact, you wouldn't mind drinking cold anything right now.

Dinner will be served downstairs in fifteen minutes. You go to the closet to find the Japanese pyjamas, or kimono, which has been provided for your stay. You feel a little silly putting this on and wearing it to dinner, until you are actually in the dining room and see everyone else wearing the same thing. Now this phenomenon is no longer silly, but picture worthy. Everyone poses and snaps for five minutes.

Once you've taken off your inn slippers and are barefoot on the tatami mats, you realize why one wears a kimono to dinner. Not being used to sitting on your heels for long periods of time as it is, you really wouldn't be able to manage in jeans! The guide tells you, however, that unlike a Western hotel, which is more formal, a Japanese ryokan makes an effort to be as comfortable as home. On that note, don't be surprised seeing a group of kimono clad businessmen in the morning having beer with breakfast!

At the dinner "table" you are presented with raw beef, vegetables, tofu and steamed rice. For a minute you cringe and wonder if the Japanese eat their beef raw like their fish, until you see the skillet right in front of you .

The Japanese servers float from table to table, demonstrating how to add soy sauce and stir-fry. Don't be embarrassed if you struggle with the chopsticks. Chances are someone has asked for a fork before you.

Make sure to order a bottle of sake, the Japanese rice wine, poured warm from a small decanter into mini-teacups. The taste is not for everyone, but is worth a try to say you've "done it."

By the end of dinner you will be so full that crawling out the dining room seems like an appealing option. Remembering that the public bath on the lower level of the inn awaits you, however, floating in the naturally warm hot spring water sounds even better.

This experience of sharing a bath with other members of the same sex will only make you uncomfortable if you are terribly modest. Even then, the idea of soaking tired feet and muscles in such a relaxed environment, second nature to the Japanese, should make you ease up and embrace the experience for culture's sake.

After removing the inn slippers and depositing your kimono into a cubby-hole, enter the spa area nude. Here you will find several removable showerheads and soap to clean your body first before immersing yourself into the shared bath. Ahhhhh.

Ascending the stairs fully relaxed (and prune-like) back to your room, you may eye the vending machine full of Japanese beer, and mental note it for later. A personal futon and down comforter awaits you inside. And when you finally lie down, it nearly feels like you're lying on air.

The following morning you can choose to have breakfast brought to your room or head downstairs to the tatami mats. Don't expect to see eggs and bacon, or anything else you might recognize for that matter. Instead, prepare to encounter a tray with many small dishes: steamed rice, miso soup with bamboo shoots, seaweed soup with tofu, sesame spinach, fishcakes (think hotdog, but with fish), raw fish and eggplant. If you're not culinary adventuresome, this may be a morning you wish a McDonald's isn't far away!

At checkout you will feel like you have been immersed in Japanese culture in a way which is unlike visiting temples and seeing other sights. It is almost sad to turn in those brown, worn slippers for your everyday shoes.

MEETING OBA YAA
Susanna Mullard

As I first stepped off the plane in Ghana on January 19th, 2001, I was met by a wave of hot, humid, tropical air. I'd been working to raise money for five months since leaving school, and to have finally arrived in Africa felt incredible - I had to pinch myself to realise the dream had become a reality. There was an indefinable buzz in the air, and as I was swept along by the hustles of people at the airport, I could not help but smile.

After an extremely bumpy forty-minute drive through the Ghanaian streets, lined with lantern-lit stalls trading fruit and spices, the Teaching and Projects Abroad representative dropped me off at my host's house in Teshie Nungua, a small residential area outside the capital, Accra. My Ghanaian 'mother,' Oba Yaa, met me outside her large, tatty house surrounded by jungle and shanty town, threw her arms around me and said, "My blonde lady, come with me." From that moment I felt completely at home and knew that this was to be the amazing experience I had hoped for. I hardly slept that night, in part because I could not work out how to operate the ceiling fan, but also because I was filled with anticipation and excitement for what was to come.

In the following five months, I progressively fell in love with Ghana, as it continued to exceed my expectations and challenge the way I thought. I was teaching at Adu Memorial School, one of the poorest in the neighbourhood, but undoubtedly the friendliest. Teaching came as quite a challenge: you never fully appreciate how hard the job is until you do it yourself — especially when your classroom consists of four walls of scrap wood nailed together with forty children squeezed inside, too poor to afford paper, let alone shoes. It was stiflingly hot, and I had to avoid the potholes on the floor as I taught, explaining a particular exercise to a class of all different ages and abilities - one child may be able to write a GCSE level essay, while another could not even pick up a pencil.

However, despite the surrounding poverty, the atmosphere was one of overwhelming joy and faith in humanity, and the people were the happiest I had ever come across. The children have such spirit and soul to them, and everywhere I walked I was surrounded by children tugging on my arms, crying, "Auntie Suzie, Auntie Suzie!", trying to rub off the white from my alien Caucasian skin, convinced I would be black underneath. I have found out that many of them are orphans, and slept on the classroom floor at night, and would have to be thrown out of the school if they could not pay their fees. So, after receiving a donation from a family friend who had read one of my e-mails back home, I managed to pay the annual fees for 12 students.

My final month in Ghana was spent working in the local SOS orphanage in Tema, the next city along the coastline to the east of Accra. Like all SOS establishments, the orphans were divided up into families of all different ages, each looked after by their own village mother in houses scattered around the campus. I was allocated to help Mother Gertie in 'House Grandma Alice' and my special responsibility was to care for two three-month-old twin babies who had been abandoned by their parents. They were more than a handful, and I found myself going home on the tro tro (an ancient bus that should have failed its MOT 20 years ago) every day covered in baby sick and food. Yet, the experience as a whole was extremely moving, especially seeing how the mothers sacrificed their lives to care for the orphans, and what an exceptional start in life the children were given.

My home life living with the Afrifa family was as eventful as any other part of my trip, and it was the warmth of the Ghanaian people that made my stay such a happy one. After walking home from school down the orange dirt road, with multi-coloured lizards crossing my path, and carrying my piles of marking, I would be met by the Afrifa family and their friends, with shouts of "Abruni, akwaaba!" ("welcome home white girl"). Living with a huge extended family, we would spend our afternoons washing in the courtyard, playing with the children and perfecting the local 'Twi' language, while in the evenings we went out to local bars, perfecting the art of climbing the eight foot fence surrounding the house at 1am, followed by swinging from the mango tree outside my room.

Through time I discovered that Oba Yaa Afrifa, my host mother, was in fact one of the main political figures in Ghana, going on regular trips to the Volta Region, her constituency. Her husband had been executed by Rawlings during the coup, and she now had close alliances with the President of Ghana, J. Kuffour. Her promise to introduce us to him never quite materialized, but she was extremely well respected in the neighbourhood, and everybody knew who we were due to the fact that we were staying with her. It was great fun playing the local celebrity!

Each day in Ghana was different from the next and brought new challenges and experiences. Coco Beach was a ten-minute walk away, a breathtaking expanse of white sand and palm trees, with Rastafarians walking up and down selling jewellery. One day we decided to walk up the beach to reach the next village, but as the tide came in we found ourselves unable to turn back, and instead were forced to climb up into the shantytown above us. I thought I had seen poverty in my surroundings, but nothing had ever prepared me for this. However, even in the face of adversity the Ghanaians kept smiling.

I was fortunate enough to spend my weekends and holidays travelling around Ghana with the other volunteers. Tourism in Ghana is still quite under-developed, so every experience felt very unique and unobtrusive, which made it even more special. The climax of the tour, however, was sleeping under the stars on safari in Mole National Park, covered only by a mosquito net, after spending three hours following a herd of elephants with our guide.

My time in Ghana really was the mind-opening and challenging experience I had hoped for. There were times of shock and despair (the Accra Sports Stadium Disaster being one of these), and settling into life in a Third World country was at first challenging. Nevertheless, after already returning last Christmas, I know I will do so again at every available opportunity.

A good traveller is one who does not know where he is going to, and a perfect traveller does not know where he came from.
Lin Yutang. The Importance of Living

"People will forget what you said. People will forget what you did. But people will never forget how you make them feel." Anon

PARIS IN THE SPRINGTIME
Dawn Slaughter

" I love Paris in the springtime." Okay, so January is not technically spring but comparing the dark, windy, cold world of St Andrews I had left behind with an un-seasonally sunny Paris, permits me a little blurring of the seasons. Besides, I am one of those hopeless romantics who loves Paris at any time of the year. Each time I return she never fails to offer up something new from her extensive a la carte menu. This time I had broken my previous Paris city break code, ditched the other half and prised a good girlfriend from hers. Thus, as two de facto singletons we landed in one of Europe's most bohemian centres ready to let off pent up exam, or in her case, cranky boss, pressure. (I'd like to pause for thought at this point just to thank the wonderful *Ryan Air* for allowing us poor student types to do this sort of thing at the drop of a beret as it were. My return flight was a whisker off £25 - it costs more for a return train journey from Leuchars to Inverness. I know where I'd rather be. Wouldn't it be interesting to ask the MD when he will just be done with it and give the flights away?)

The said girlfriend and I had made a pact to avoid Paris's clichés, our whistle stop definition of what we actually meant by that ran more or less like this:

1. No two hour queues to go up the Eiffel Tower, only to be conned into buying one of those luminous sticky men that wriggle their way down walls like slugs.

2. No gawping at the *Mona Lisa* surrounded by hoards of clicking Japanese tourists taking photos despite the "No photographs" sign in every conceivable language.

3. No getting ripped-off in cafés claiming one or another genius artist, philosopher or poet once, at some point or another, in his long life drank there as justification for a *café au lait* costing 10 euros.

Paris being Paris, we quickly realised that we'd embarked on mission impossible. She is not the type to allow her notoriety to be diluted. She knows that just as a great actress lives and breaths her highs, lows, loves and experiences, thus becoming legendary through her flaws as well as her perfections, great cities are great because they revel in their scandals, their clichés, as well as their *coté chic*: Think of Marilyn Monroe; we all know she wasn't perfect, yet she is loved the world over. We never tire of the white dress over the air vent picture, or the *Happy Birthday* song. Now think Paris, we love *Montmatre* and *The Moulin Rouge* because of their well worn seediness. Many of us balk at the idea of actually swallowing an escargot or a slice of *foie gras*, yet isn't it wonderful that such delicacies persist in our pre-packed, globalized,

politically correct age? Now think Alicia Silverstone, the epitome of the ubiquitous bubbly blonde next door- beautiful yes, but when it comes down to it, rather boring. Rather like, say Brussels; she plays her role to a tee but in never

daring to wander where she shouldn't and remaining PC, she instantly becomes forgettable. Doomed to their respective niche - the romantic interest and the terminally practical political centre.

Upon opening our eyes to Paris in all her familiar glory we thus witnessed, on full display, some of her rather more unfortunate stereotypes: the bad drivers, for example. As a child I have the hellish memory of circling round and round the *Arc de Triomphe* as a friend's father tried in vain to exit amongst a shower of screaming horns. (Which wise bureaucrat decided that those entering the roundabout should have priority over those exiting? Answers on a postcard please.) This time the proof came in the form of a couple of gendarmes, some firemen and a hapless motorist or two, staring at the remnants of a sad looking Renault twingo and a moped. Further investigation confirmed that almost every car in Paris has a bump, scratch or scrape somewhere on the bodywork.

Another cliché must be the inevitably disgruntled waiter: let's face it, any francophone has lived this one a few more times than they'd care to remember, but it seems Paris breeds a special sub-species of her own. Never before have I been told "dépechez-vous" over a chocolate mousse or asked to pay up because my waiter had a date that night! After these two little incidents within a few hours of arriving in Paris, as well as finding our youth hostel just around the corner from Notre Dame (we couldn't possibly not try and catch a glimpse of Quasimodo) and not forgetting several skinny 40-somethings tottering along the pavement, perfectly preened pooches in hand, we decided that trying to avoid the clichés in Paris is like trying to avoid pashmina shawls in St Andrews. Impossible. Indeed, not only can't it be done, the week-ender must accept it as part of the course, revel in its inevitability and smile at the comforting feeling it inspires. Being in Paris for a break with a good friend should be like watching all the best bits of Jean-Pierre Jeanet's "Le Fabuleux destin d'Amelie Poulain". It should make you laugh out loud, feel giddy, shed a tear, but most of all make you love life. With this in mind we spent our days revelling in the world of the many easy pleasures Paris has to offer. We ate crepes stuffed with the ubiquitous nutella, had our portraits drawn at *Montmatre*, strolled through the *Quartier Latin*, and even found time to catch a typically thought provoking French film about Alzheimer's disease (Se Souvenir de Belles Choses). Some little treasure to note for another visit must begin with a little café called "Le Paradis de Fruits" which has an uninterrupted view over the Seine and Notre Dame and offers an endless menu of freshly squeezed juices - I'd especially recommend the unctuous strawberry, raspberry and lychee option. Another is a tiny scruffy looking sandwich bar tucked up a side street in *Montmatre* where the cheerful waiter offers an optional dancing lesson as desert after your filled baguette. Visitors swarm like bees to the lavender of Provence towards the stunning boulevards and monuments of Paris; the trick is to smile with her as she revels in the attention and blossoms like a film star, resplendent under the relentless glare of the clicking cameras.

I'M IN INDIA: A SELECTION OF E-MAILS
Kasia Davies

Sunday, 05 Nov 2000. Subject: I'm in India.
Dear Everyone,

There's no turning back now, I'm in a hotel in Trivandrum and it feels as if I'm melting. It's not that hot but it's so humid that it feels like a sauna. I'm not going to the school until tomorrow - a four-hour train ride starting at five in the morning. I was so tired by the time we landed last night that I thought I would be glad of a break from travel, but in fact I just want to get there now. The main problem is that I can't sleep, I'm so nervous about this trip, so I've been awake for about 36 hours non-stop. The muggy atmosphere has affected my appetite; I can't seem to stomach food, so I think my body must be in shock. I'm feeling rather sorry for myself, I suppose it's because I'm alone and it's all so very strange. I will feel better when I've been taken under the wing of the school principal, met the children, and unpacked in my new room. Then I'll know what I'm doing and it will only be a few days until the other English volunteer, Beth, arrives to keep me company.

The colours: off-white and dirty yellow buildings, enormously tall green palm trees, brightly coloured political posters plastered everywhere and the gleaming brown bodies of tiny men who wear nothing but short skirts, Roman style. The sounds: auto-rickshaws honking, the odd snatch of Indian singing, and some exotic loud birds. The smells: a few wafts from the kitchen below my room, citronella oil to ward of mosquitoes, refreshing peppermint soap, and just a general air of sticky hot damp. The tastes: cotton wool toast washed down with tea that I was brave enough to eat this morning, and a permanent salty tang in my mouth, although I'm drinking lots of water – bottles or filtered of course. As for my sense of touch there is only one word – *clammy.*

Wed, 15 Nov, 2000.
Dear Everyone,

At five in the morning I boarded the train packed with people commuting to work. Many were travelling more than 10 hours to their place of work and would spend the week there. I had three hours on the wooden seats, which became more cramped at every station; the Indians will always squeeze up for one more person. It was the most interesting train ride ever. The carriages were open so that the cool morning breezes could rush in and I was able to get the most of the amazing landscape. In Kerala slums aren't common because everyone has their own piece of land and a one-room coconut leaf shack. The backwaters are truly a tropical Venice, with floating islands of lush greenery in a network of intricate canals. I received the usual polite questioning from passengers, men came up and down the carriage with tea and coffee and before I knew it we were in the village of Mavelikara, where the principal and his chauffer were waiting.

The region was originally mostly paddy fields, but now they import their rice from Tamil Nadu, as the Keralites are too educated nowadays to lower themselves to working in them. The school is on a slight hill overlooking these. It seems tranquil and cool compared to the dust and noise of Trivandrum, but still very hot. My room is in the hostel where teachers and boarders live. There is a wonderful community atmosphere, the teachers are young and the children are very playful and affectionate. I'm rarely alone as they follow me like a herd of ducklings, firing questions, asking to take photos and giving me presents varying from melting kit-kat bars to paper flowers. They remember every detail about their English guests but the fact that I'm a young lone female adds value to the novelty. Their favourite request is for me to sing or tell them a story and they themselves are natural performers, despite their modesty. They all know the *Titanic* theme tune by heart, mimicking Celine Dion perfectly and they also do some incredible breakdancing to Hindi music; the dancers on *Top of the Pops* are talent - less by comparison.

Kerela is definitely a good, if slightly gentle introduction to India. Its health system is so good that they've completely eradicated malaria; the seventy pounds worth of malaria tablets I bought are therefore redundant. The 100% literacy rate means that competition for jobs is huge and everyone has a string of qualifications. The school children study very hard, spending four to six hours a day doing homework, boarders up at five and to bed by ten-thirty; it is a strict and regimented life. Their other pre-occupation, apart from education, is religion. Their principal's first question was "what is your denomination?" My smart answer was that I was a member of the human race. Hymns and prayers can be heard throughout the day. They also keep asking to hear our national anthem; they of course know theirs off by heart and sing it every day.

Fri 1 Dec 2000
Dear Everyone,

It seems to have been a crazy week here as nothing has gone as we had expected. For a start the weather has taken us by surprise because it has been awful: we've had power cuts that last between six and sixteen hours. The generator is very irregular. It sometimes works for part of the day then cuts out in the evening, so then we have to resort to candles or torches. This also means that the fans can't operate so the air becomes very still and humid between the storms but then when the rain does come it tends to cool down. There are terrific displays of thunder and lightning, too. The school grounds are flooding because the ground is so hard and it doesn't absorb the water and the roads seem to have turned into rusty rivers. Everywhere in Mabelkira people can be seen with black umbrellas. Wading in their flip-flops or going barefoot, no one stops for the weather. Apparently the electricity lines have been damaged so power cuts may continue.

Other news is that last week we were invited by a pupil to accompany her to the family temple where they were having a festival. We went with her after school by bus and since the roads have no drains it was ankle deep in water. It also had to swerve to avoid the cyclist and their umbrellas so we likened the experience to a combination of the log flume and runaway train rides at *Alton Towers*. Finally we got there and were given tea. We had the most delicious homemade samosas I have ever tasted and sweet milky coffee. There isn't any temple building since the whole site is considered sacred and you enter through a huge archway, lit with thousands of fairy lights, into an area that they compared to the playgrounds of the Gods. To us it seemed like a huge funfair at night because everything was lit so brightly; there were stalls of sweets, fruit, cloth and souvenirs everywhere and loud religious music blaring out from stages where musicians gathered. We took our sandals off and squelched through the puddles with everyone else. There was a mixture of people: elderly pilgrims, dressed in white, beggars sleeping under the trees, violinists who could be commissioned to play a song to protect you from the snakes, and families standing to pray. The trees themselves were beautifully old, their trunks were a tangle of twisted branches, so you couldn't tell how many trees there were. Old oil lamps or painted idols of gods were hanging form them. The atmosphere was extraordinary; religion has never been so exciting!

Fri 8th Dec 200
Dear Everyone,

Last weekend we went to Cochin and it was a great success. I managed to keep myself occupied on the three-and-a-half hour train journey with a book of Chekhov's plays borrowed from the school library. I would recommend *The Seagull* and *The Three Sisters*. We wanted to see how little we could spend if we chose all the budget options so we stayed in a YMCA economy room, which was fine except that the huge windows had no curtains so we woke at dawn. Fortunately, we still had the energy to see all the sights. On Saturday, we took the ferry across the harbour, past all the Indian Army Ships, to Fort Cochi. This small but historic Island has two famous churches and a quiet little beach. In the evening we went to see a *Kathalaki* play. This is a traditional style theatre unique to Kerela. We sat in a coconut shack, as several actors presented a story about the antics of Hindu gods. They wore richly coloured costumes, extraordinary face paint and were rolling their eyes strangely. Our verdict: confusing but entertaining.

Fri 29th Dec 2000.
Dear Everyone,

The big event at the school was the Christmas function on the ninth. In the morning there was the carol service, in which we had to read a lesson each. In the afternoon there was a three hour-long performance, in which every year of the school had an opportunity to display their talent. The dances were amazing: tiny children doing the foot stamping traditional dances, older girls doing sexy film routines and the boys doing comic acting dances. All this, as well as a good dose of festive spirit, with a cashew nut Christmas tree and Santa Claus distributing sweets to all the children at the end combined for a splendid evening.

Tue, 02 Jan 2001
Dear Everyone,

Happy New Year.
Obviously the world still hasn't ended yet despite all Nostradamus's predictions, but from the noise and flashes of fire that were produced by the

34

Indians letting off highly dangerous fireworks at midnight it did seem as if it might be.

Wed, 10 Jan 2001
Dear Everyone,

Where do I start: we stood for two hours on the bus getting here; it was dark by the time we arrived and every hotel seemed to be full: three rickshaws and a dozen hotels later we did find somewhere on the edge of town but it was rather dodgy and the porter stalked us for the next two days. Yes that's right, he stood outside our room for hours at a time and every time we opened the door he'd come up with some excuse for being there. It would have been bearable if we'd had lots to do outside but it poured with rain the whole two days we were there. I had a dodgy stomach and neither Beth nor I could get much sleep because there were rats scratching in the roof above me. I ventured out on several occasions desperately trying to find something to like and keep myself occupied, alas I never did. The weather was certainly grey and dismal enough to be French, the shops all closed for three hours at lunchtime in their annoyingly French way, and there was even a few ludicrously expensive cafes pretending to be French; so I guess the only element missing was the fact that, whereas France fascinates and stimulates me, Pondicherry just bored and frustrated me. We were keen to leave, so not at all put off to find that the next train out left at four in the morning.

Tues. 16th Jan 2002.
Dear Everyone,

It has been a fairly standard week here but on the weekend we indulged ourselves with a visit to the beach. This time it was Varkala. It's paradise and only two hours down the road. We shared an umbrella with a bunch of Israelis - the largest travelling nationality in India, followed by the Brits and the Germans.

Wed 31 Jan 2002.

Apart from the gorgeous views from the bus on the way to Peryar wildlife sanctuary, I did not have a very successful weekend. We had to queue for hours, only to find that the tickets had sold out. Eventually, when we made it into the sanctuary, we discovered that the resident elephants were enjoying a Sunday lie-in. We were very disappointed but consoled ourselves with a big breakfast, which the monkeys tried to steal. We also had a chat with an Indian tourist who informed us that Britain has no wildlife. When we tried to tell him that we may not have tigers we do have deer, badgers, foxes, etc. He replied, "Oh but they're only stray animals - not big enough to be really *wild*." So it's a good thing we went to Peryar and enjoyed the privilege of seeing pigs.

This brings to me onto my next topic: common Indian misconceptions about Britain. We are frequently asked the following questions:

-How can you survive as vegetarian when it is too cold to grow fruit and vegetables?

-How do you wash in winter when the water is so cold?

-How do you get drinking water if you don't have a well in your gar den?

-Will your parents be annoyed or worried if you don't have a boy friend by a certain age?

My favourite theory came from the principle, Mr Cherian, who proudly announced that westerners don't eat with their hands: "because the water is too cold to wash your hands before and after meals."

Fri 16th Feb

Dear Everyone,

Yesterday we had another little chat with Mr Cherian, in which he asked us for the umpteenth time whether we would like him to arrange Indian bridegrooms for us next time we come to India. I explained that, while I might fall in love with an Indian, I would still prefer not to have an arranged marriage. He then proceeded to draw a graph with the amount of time along one axis and level of happiness along the other. According to him happiness increases gradually over time in an arranged marriage, but decreases steadily after a love marriage. This because in a love marriage the couple have all the enjoyment of getting to know each other before the weeding and afterwards they only find out the bad aspects of each other. I tried to suggest that couples in love could go on finding joy in each other after marriage, because they had chosen to spend the rest of their lives together. But he flatly told me this was against all the laws of physics and mathematics.

Tues Feb 2001
Dear Everyone,

In my last few days of teaching I have felt more depressed than I could ever have imagined about leaving. Yesterday I sang, "if you're happy and you know it" with tears running down my cheeks.

Things will be different now as I embark on a great expedition round India, new places and faces all the time. First stop Goa. We stayed away from the most touristy places where the package holiday makers go, but you could still spot them a mile off: their shorts and sandals looked too new, they didn't know how to bargain and they couldn't understand the menus. It was strange to think they'd only visit India for a week or two and all they'd see would be the beach. It felt like an artificial place, with no real community. The Goan men in particular were very disagreeable; they were so lazy and would spend all day making crude comments as you walked past. The most dominating presence on the beach was the huge number of sellers: little children and young women selling the usual trinkets and souvenirs to sunbathers. Also many courting couples came down from the city to stroll along the beach and the men would ask their girlfriends to take photos of them posing next to the girls in bikinis.

We had no regrets to leave Goa behind. Although gorgeous, we could not accept such a hedonistic lifestyle for more than a week. Bombay was incredible, I never expected to enjoy a city so much. Colonial rule has left a strong mark on the city in the form of Georgian and Victorian buildings, and red double-decker buses. Even the train station where we arrived seemed just like Paddington.

Mon, 19th March 2001
Dear Everyone,

Indian food is driving me crazy. It all tastes the same. I prefer South Indian food. I'd rather have rice all day than chapattis and Naan bread. I'm tired of going to restaurant three times a day, ordering form the same list of items – I have cravings for lettuce and broccoli. I think I will go on a diet: tangerines, banana porridge, and omelettes. This must be a sign its time to come home.

HAMPI, SOUTHERN INDIA
Nicola Shipway

The ancient city of Hampi - the alleged birth-place of Shiva the Hindu god of destruction and rejuvenation - is considered holy. It is neither a glamorous nor a restful destination, but for those in the south of India it offers the opportunity to explore a site of religious and historic importance, unaffected by any Western influence other than Coca-Cola. Situated in the central Karnataka region, the city boasts spectacular ruins dating from the middle of the fifteenth century.

Hampi, traditionally named Vijayanagar, was deserted after the destructive Muslim wars of 1565. It remained so until 1856 when a British explorer rediscovered it, Indiana Jones style, overrun by tigers and monkeys. Today the town is bustling and thriving, with several restaurants and a proliferation of shops, including one that sells marbled papers more associated with Florentine than Indian tradition. It is remote, and the nearest station, Hospet, is a forty-five minutes rickshaw-ride away. So potholed was the road and so possessed the driver that my knees were bruised, having been forcibly rammed against the seats in front.

Our guesthouse was sociably filled with travellers, cost only forty rupees per night, and was painted a magnificent turquoise. The relaxed atmosphere ensured that it was a hippy haven, with a one-sink courtyard overshadowed by a dove-bedecked tree.

The ruins of Hampi are so extensive that we engaged a guide, who proved to be invaluable. We spent two days wandering around temples and palaces over five hundred years old, and walked over eight kilometres on the first day. The interior of one temple was originally adorned with gold and diamonds, and the pornographic images around the walls were intended to detract the onlooker from remarking upon this opulence. It was considered that dwelling on such earthly beauty brought about its destruction.

Fairy tale magnificence abounded elsewhere: the Queen's fountain had been studded with rubies and emeralds. One of the Queen's Palaces was made up of hundreds of stone columns supporting a ceiling, the architectural form contrived simply to create music. During celebrations each column was tapped with silver sticks covered in beeswax, and with the aid of curtains rather than walls to keep out the wind the music carried for miles.

We walked around the foundations of one palace that had been made of sandalwood, and was famous for its scent. Nearby stood the elephant stables, housing eleven animals in a grandeur unparalleled anywhere in India. The king was known as the husband of elephants, symbolising his strength, majesty and peace-loving proclivities. He was so loved that many subjects presented themselves for service as eunuch soldiers. Their testicles were ritually removed with knives slammed onto wooden plates, but their sacrifice earned them the King's protection. Women also suffered, for the city famously practised *sati*, and widows were commonly burned on their husband's funeral pyres.

Our tour continued on the second day, this time on bicycle. We saw paddy fields and kingfishers, lush banana groves and carts selling crushed sugar cane. We ate papaya and were told that if eaten too green it induced miscarriages in pregnancies up to three months old, which accounted for the fact that married women did not eat it. We admired delicate mimosa flowers, known locally as 'shy Indian girls' because their leaves modestly close up when touched. Our cosmopolitan guide boasted of his more famous clients, and recalled how Bruce Willis had declared the landscape to be 'f**king amazing'. It was too: the granite is as smooth as a skull, the hairy grasses common to dry climates somehow shorn to reveal the hard, bone-like rock beneath. *The Lonely Planet* calls it 'almost magical', and it is perceived as such. Every so often we would pass 'wishing houses', where people had constructed tiny arches using three small stones, dedicated to fulfilling the architect's desire.

Hampi is a city throbbing with history, and the very landscape exudes a monumentality that is awe-inspiring. India is renowned for its spirituality, but I saw more bald and scarlet-clad saddhus meditating beneath boulders in Hampi than anywhere else in the peninsula. Accordingly, the rickshaw journey should be braved at all costs.

"Two roads diverged in a wood, and I took the one less travelled by, and that has made all the difference."
Robert Frost

"Whatever you say about India, the opposite is also true."
Anon

THE UGANDAN BUSH
Alice Rawdon-Mogg

Monday 13th August.

Our first morning in Uganda!

We arrived in darkness yesterday evening for our first taste of Africa. The bus that took us off to our base camp was 1970s - style and the three hour journey took us through Kampala past hundreds of shacks, most of which looked like shops with wide open doors and people relaxing outside. There were petrol stations, one of which we stopped at to refuel and relieve ourselves behind a rather small bush, in spite of the two men guarding the petrol station with shotguns. A mouse scampered across my foot – rather tame I thought for a piece of African wildlife. We spent the first hour of the journey singing and gazing out of the window. Some people in other vehicles responded with songs or waves. The driving was surprisingly hasty until we discovered that the driver's reluctance to slow down and refusal to stop at a roadblock was because the area was renowned for hijacks. When we arrived we were shown our beds and given some soup. Very soon my head hit the sack.

The next morning we awoke to see the camp in its entirety, views and all. Wow! The camp is right next to the River Nile in the district of Jinja. Looking out into the river you can see the other bank in the distance; the river itself forms an impressive set of rapids just below the camp – a huge mass of surging water. There are several other little islands just upstream of the rapids, all covered in dense vegetation – home for hundreds of birds. The morning brought the opportunity to test out the shower. A highly effective contraption consisting of a bucket with holes in it which, after pouring some water into it, is winched up and you then stand underneath. We even have warm water!

This morning was quite a slow, lazy morning, recovering from the previous day's travel. I had rather an amusing conversation with a local guy who could not understand why white people wanted to tan their skin. After being briefed about our intended itinerary and all the practicalities of life here, we all jumped on the Land Rover and headed towards Jinja. This must have been an amusing sight – fourteen people crammed into the back of a vehicle. About halfway there, we stopped in a village to visit a couple of the locals, including a 'Head Man' and the local madman who is an old war veteran. While we stopped, all the children emerged and stood in shy crowds staring at us. After a while they grew bold and edged closer, laughing and waving at us. The journey to Jinja was our first real experience of the local area. Every hut and village we went past had screaming and waving children – the expressions of sincere and pure delight at seeing a 'musungu' (white man). We spent the entire journey waving at every man, woman and child. Once we arrived in Jinja, there was half an hour to wander around before we had to go back. The people in the town were far more passé about the 'musungu' and we were able to wander around more freely. We found a market that sold just about everything; including a local delicacy - white ants that looked like fried earwigs!

Half of us travelled back to a camp in a taxi (a mini camper van cum minibus), which involves putting your life on the line. Having arrived safely back, we discovered that the camp had attracted huge crowds of local children and adults. We began to talk to them and ended up showing them Ceilidh dancing with pipes, playing Frisbee, and skipping (once we had plaited a rope). Despite the language barrier between most of the children and ourselves, we were able to communicate and they all highly enjoyed themselves and the interaction we all experienced is beyond words. The worst aspect was having to keep all the children a distance away from the camp. It's just not fair to give them the temptation of all out kit to steal, especially as they are so friendly and keen and wouldn't normally contemplate stealing – out kit provides a higher degree of temptation and the authorities are very harsh on those who steal from white people as it might discourage tourism.

Tuesday 14th August.
On return to the camp after a busy day on the river, in a smaller group than usual, we discovered that a huge crowd of children had formed. Because there were so few of us they were less timid than usual. Once I responded to a "hello, how are you?" a crowd of approximately fifty kids quickly surrounded me. More and more of them grew bold enough to ask questions such as "how are you," what our names were and where we came from. Some of them were so shy they threw themselves on the ground or ran away as soon as they had spoken. One of them stuck out his hand for me to shake. Once I had done this I had every hand in sight shoved into mine. It was quite intimidating to begin with, but I soon relaxed. I have to admit that my eyes filled with tears at one point because of their intense and sincere joy at such simple gestures.

Wednesday 15ᵗʰ August.

After major preparations we set off on a two-day kayaking trip along the Nile. A hair-raising drive took us towards the river along a track, which would not even qualify as a footpath back in Britain. We all helped to load our kit onto a large, wooden canoe- a local taxi- and it was carried across to our home for the night, a small, uninhabited island. Despite this location, the trend continued and a few locals turned up every now and then to see if they could sell us anything. After a day on the river, which proved to be a great learning experience, I retired for the evening feeling half drowned to sit around the fire and watch the sun go down.

Thursday 16ᵗʰ August.

I woke first and enjoyed a delicious breakfast of scrambled eggs on toast. Slowly, everybody emerged, packed away 'Camp Cloud' and set off on the 6km trek down the river in kayaks. Before long, we stopped to sample the local drink Warragi (distilled sugar cane, banana and goodness knows what else!) after which I had plenty of Dutch Courage to tackle the forthcoming rapids.

Our kayaks fascinated the locals and we allowed them to try them out during one of our rest stops. They had a great time fooling around, falling in and laughing at us failing to paddle their wooden dugout canoes. I was able to show off my new skill, namely Eskimo rolling. They then followed us down the river working very hard to keep up with our streamlined, lightweight boats – I think they were trying to catch a 'musungu' wife!

After attacking the rapids several times, (and paddling past some na-ked men in the middle of washing their clothes in the river) we landed and wolfed down a spicy lunch under the surveillance of hundreds of local eyes. Back at the camp for a well-earned rest, I had a conversation with Isaac, one of the locals working for Tayforth, which progressed from differing marriage traditions to learning some of his language and discussing the local children's reactions to us.

Friday 17ᵗʰ August.

Four of us were selected to start on the Military Aid to a Civilian Community (MACC) task, early this morning. Two of us were dropped off in each village. In my case, we were by a well at the edge of a village in the middle of no-where. We had a Busoga Trust technician, Sam, with us and we soon got to know the main characters amidst the crowd of villagers that had gathered to help. It was a bit intimidating to begin with, I have to admit, when the Land Rover drove off leaving us alone in such unfamiliar surroundings. However, the villagers were so friendly that we were soon able to communicate with both those who spoke English and the majority who did not. Certain characters soon emerged: Peter, an ex-Ugandan army veteran and village joker, approximately thirty-five years old, and Muhammad, a Muslim school teacher with very good English who was very keen on having an English pen-pal – surprise, surprise!

The well had been dug in 1991 by a charity called 'Water Aid' who had then relocated and went off leaving seven or eight wells in the area uncompleted and hazardous for children and animals. Over the ten years since, the wells have become putrid and contaminated with everything imaginable and some things better off left unimagined! Our job therefore, is to pump the well dry, scrub and disinfect them and remove all the rubbish. Then, we have to build a couple of soakaway trenches, one of which is concreted and bricked, in order to channel all water spillages away and prevent it from recontaminating the well again. A raised wall needs to be built around the well and the concrete slab, which has been lying next to the well for ten years, placed on top. A conversion frame will be concreted on because we will use a different type of pump to the U3 they planned to use in 1991. Finally, a fence needs to be built around the well site in order to keep animals out and to mark off the area as a clean area.

When we first arrived the villagers were already busy breaking up stones by hand for the aggregate, so we soon joined in. The morning passed with the well being pumped and cleared and a huge pile of stones being broken up. At about 12.30 a cup of hugely milky tea arrived for us along with some dried beans produced by the villagers. We were taken off and sat under a mango tree with banana leaves covering the ground for us. Soon after this break, a sociologist called Joseph arrived on a motorbike and we went with him to interview and inspect the villagers' homesteads. This was an experience that is difficult to put into words. We looked at the kitchen areas, washing facilities and latrines. Several homesteads had the traditional type of latrine - a pit latrine - which is supposed to start off 10ft deep and should last a family of five to six people approximately two years. However, many were badly constructed, with little shelter around the edges or even a roof. Some homesteads did not even have this and simply used the 'garden' (bushes surrounding the buildings). Many of the kitchens did not have smoke vents and had rickety old roofs with firewood stored hazardously among the support beams, or rather, sticks. The plates and cups were scattered around the mud floors in the circular wooden and mud huts with dried banana leaf roofs. One even had goat droppings scattered amidst potato peelings, etc. where the goats had been roaming freely. The villagers had developed bad habits such as washing their plates inside and throwing the water on the floor. Very few had the suggested plate racks (a simple wooden structure) and those that did were accused of 'rack abuse' by Joseph because of the lack of soakaway pits and the presence of rusty corrugated iron contaminating the plates once they had been washed. Similarly, there were few refuse pits and the list of issues brought up by Joseph is endless. He was rightly adamant that it is a God-given right for every human to have privacy for washing and relieving themselves – therefore a six foot shelter for washing with a proper drainage system was absolutely necessary. Not a single household had this. None of the people boiled their water on a regular basis and very few washed the clay pots used for storing drinking water more often than about once every 6 months. We looked for evidence of hand washing facilities. One family had this, no others, although it was clear that the word had gone round while we were interviewing and bottles began to randomly and suspiciously appear. These things are all physical and practical aspects of this experience – it is difficult to describe the impact of seeing these malnourished children with potbellies, bald patches and eye infections. I found it hugely frustrating.

Before we left the village, the remaining villagers around the well entertained us by singing their national anthem; a man appeared with a local musical instrument, a wooden box with strategically placed metal bars, which were 'twanged' to produce a very mellow sound. What an end to our first day experiencing the grim reality of these rural communities.

Saturday 18th August.
The weekend had arrived, so there were many more children around. By lunchtime they had grown brave enough to try out their English and shake us by the hand. We were given lunch under the same tree as yesterday only this time we had a banana based dish, 'matoke,' with the same meat (but without the abdominal wall lining this time). I had a rather embarrassing moment choking with the meat on account of its toughness; I hope they were not too offended. At around 2.00 it started to pour with rain. There was a mad rush to cover the concrete with banana leaves and before we went back to camp we were each presented with a pineapple from Muhammad's land – something to remind us of him.

Once reunited with the rest of the group, we set off for an evening at the Jinja Nile Resort. It turned out to have the potential for an idyllic evening, with one major flaw. It had a beautiful view overlooking the Nile, a large swimming pool, a bar and sun-loungers. The problem was the contrast between the village that we had spent the day in and the gross amount of wealth that now surrounded us. Despite this, the evening progressed well.

Monday 20ᵗʰ August.

We had a morning at the well site without the technician and both groups managed to make the same mistake. We had been told that a soakaway pit needed to be dug and this seemed simple enough – how hard can it be? Well, that's what we thought until we discovered that the exact spot that we had decided to dig out was the site of a former well. No wonder there were so many bricks in the mud and the hole was filling up with water so quickly! After pushing the villagers into having enough motivation to dig in the first place, we now had to persuade them to fill it in again. It was looking half respectable by the time Sam-the technician-arrived. We had also managed to finish the fence and some of the brickwork around the well itself. We managed to achieve a lot considering we were without technical guidance but the 'little blunder' with the soakaway trench may have lost us some of the villager's trust in our abilities – we will have to work at our position a bit now, I think. I learnt a lot about interacting with these people today. I had a rather intimidating experience in which I brought out some pens and some women got overly excited and snatched the whole bundle. I learnt from this not to let anyone see the contents of my bag. Also, the men in the village are becoming rather forward both in terms of conversation and posing for photographs – one man appeared with a camera and was charging 500 shillings per shot!

Tuesday 21ˢᵗ August.

We spent the first half of the day sorting out and finishing up the dodgy soakaway pit. The original plan was to let the technician move on to the next well site while we remained to complete, slapping mud around the base of the well and finishing the cement plastering. However, the Chairman of the Well was unhappy about this (probably because of the soakaway incident) so we all stayed and moved onto the next site later. The new set of villagers seemed more motivated – probably because they had seen our work on the first well and so knew what to expect and believed we were here to finish the job. I took a few men off to cut some trees down for the fencing – this was great fun once I persuaded them to let me have a go – using a huge machete, or 'panga,' which was very satisfying apart from taking a huge chunk of skin off my hand.

Wednesday 22nd August.
Today's destination was a completely new well site – already with a hedge established around its perimeter. This proved to be a mixed blessing, as we discovered. Every man, woman and child got stuck into clearing the piles of dead trees and plants that were stacked up behind the hedge. After this we cut the hedge down to the height of a fence and added extra posts to supplement the bald patches. I joined in with the women hoeing for a time; they make it look so easy! I had a huge crowd being entertained by my efforts.

The morning was going very well until suddenly there was a huge commotion and everybody fled away from the centre of the work area. One of the villagers was having an epileptic fit. He fell off the pile of bricks he was sitting on, onto his back, and the villagers just stood at a distance and watched in silence. This was the first fit that I had ever seen and watching him writhe around on his back, frothing at the mouth, eyes rolled back and choking, was a terrifying and frustrating experience – especially as we were held back from stopping him from choking by the villagers who are terrified of epilepsy and think they can catch it by touching a fitting person. We refrained from interfering too much, as we are guests of their culture and lifestyle. However, ignoring the man was not an option for us, so we gave him some water and sent him home to rest out of the sun.

After things had settled down, we tried to explain our different reactions. They understood what we were saying, but did not believe us. They even suggested that maybe this man had a unique Ugandan disease rather than epilepsy, which could not understand. All of this discussion created a fair amount of tension – but we slowly mended the situation, after I had recovered from the intense shock.

Friday 24th August.
Today was 'Well Completion Day'. It is difficult to do this justice in a diary entry, but I try my best. The first part of the day was spent continuing the work of the day before. We were given possibly our last meal with the villagers – a breakfast of porridge with bread, which we ate under the mango tree with the woman who had cooked it and their children. The moment the first drops of water flowed from the pump, the crowd of villagers erupted – talk-

ing, singing, dancing, drums, with 'war cries' from the woman. Although we could not understand much of what they were saying, the expressions of pure, sincere happiness and appreciation said it all. They grabbed us, tied some cloth around our waists, African style (it was a real case of 'does my bum look big in this?' with the sure answer of 'yes, that's the point!') They got us to dance to the music – Peter on the drums and many voices joining in, with the other women. This moved onto a full village meeting in which each member of the Well Committee thanked us and we had a chance to say how much we had enjoyed working with them and how much we had learnt. The whole experience brought home to me the importance of clean water to these communities. I had tears in my eyes, not for the first time on this trip, and it is impossible to put into words the exact emotions and memories I will take away and treasure from these few moments.

Monday 27ᵗʰ August.

Our first day trekking began with a splendid full cooked breakfast. On a full stomach, we met our guide Azulukam and the porters and we set off on our adventure into Mount Elgon National Park. The day was hot and sticky so we went through a lot of water and sweets as we began the ascent along a gradual track. To begin with, the track passed through several villages and we were forever saying hello, or 'muembie' as it is in the local language. After a while we caught the first glance of our supper – a live chicken strapped atop a bag being carried on top of somebody's head. After lunch, we attacked the so-called 'wall of death'; which involved climbing steep rickety wooden ladders. It was interesting to see the villages laid out behind us, crops organised in a primitive, but self-sufficient manner. Our campsite was literally a small, flattened area amongst the trees perfectly shaped for our tents, a shelter for the porters and a shelter over the fire. The loos were very similar to those I saw in the villages last week: a wooden structure surrounding a shallow hole in the ground. The evening ended around the campfire listening to a detailed description from Azulukam of his local tribal customs – most notably, circumcision!

Tuesday 28ᵗʰ August.

I woke up at 6.30am to a breakfast of egg, chapattis and freshly roasted bran nuts…delicious. The route today was not too arduous and took us through a bamboo forest with plenty of vegetation like Old Man's Beard hanging from the trees – no monkeys or other wildlife seen yet though! Our main stop of the day was at a rangers hut from where we could see the camp we were heading towards. The view was spectacular, although by the time we had signed the visitors' book and refuelled ourselves; the mist had stolen it from our sight. We pressed on passing Red Hot Orchids, numerous herbs and 'Cousin It' plants and very soon arrived at our second campsite. There were splendid views across the valley, especially from the loo! The afternoon led to some explorations from the campsite. We set off, with Azulukam, for a pleasant evening walk; through a strange looking valley filled with trees that looked like overgrown pineapples with dead leaves surrounding the base – apparently they remain on the tree as insulation due to the high altitude. Our camp tonight is 3500m above sea level. The aim of the walk was to reach a splendid waterfall, which we did in good time. The remainder of the evening was spent listening to stories told by one of the porters and translated by Azulukam – one about a man who killed seven flies and a grasshopper. This area, in the mountains, experiences great spectacles of thunder and lightning.

Wednesday 29th August.
A reasonably early start began our journey to the 4321metre peak of Mount Elgon. The air was getting noticeably thin and I could hear my heart singing in my ears as it pumped the semi-oxygenated blood around my body. It was slow on the way up, especially when the mist came down, but after trekking around the edge of the volcano's basin, we made the final ascent. We actually waited a couple of hundred metres from the summit for everybody to catch up and headed for the top in a long line holding hands. The inevitable photos were taken and, after taking in the view, we headed down to a slightly more sheltered area for lunch, accompanied amusingly by a couple of buzzard eagles.

Thursday 30th August.
The challenge today was a 30km round trek across the basin of the volcano to some hot springs and back. Glacier movement had produced ridges within the basin, but you could still see the rim and clearly make out the enormity of the volcano, ten million years old. The outstretched view was of a plain with steep sides and interestingly shaped rocks bordering it. This was the most typical African view I had seen so far. There were loads of the 'pineapple-

shaped trees' to keep us company as well. Eventually, after much walking, talking and singing, we were able to spot the hot springs. The grass in the immediate area was bright green, due to the sulphur, and very noticeable from a distance. After a rather hairy river crossing we were finally able to test out these so-called 'hot springs'. The first thing that hit us was the rotten-egg smell of sulphur and the fact that the water was surprisingly hot – any hotter and it would have been uncomfortable. Needless to say, we all stripped off and leapt in for our first proper wash in a long time! The other exciting thing about this location was the fact that the river next to the springs was the Kenyan-Ugandan border. We couldn't resist a quick yet illegal visit to Kenya across the river.

The return journey was far more arduous, but definitely worth it. Azulukam pointed out a cave that he had used for smuggling coffee into Kenya, when he was fourteen, during the regime of Idi Amin. Apparently, they used to squeeze 150 people into this cave and stack the sacks of coffee beans outside to provide extra shelter. The coffee would have been sold in Kenya and the proceeds used to buy Kenyan goods, which would then be brought back.

Tuesday 4th September.
Today was our first day of real freedom and independence. The majority of the group have flown back to the UK, leaving five of us behind, and we now have a week of unstructured, uncontrolled adventure ahead!

Wednesday 5th September.
We were the first up at the campsite and soon set off on the 1km walk to the main road where we planned to hail down a *matato* to take us into Jinja. This we did, and we soon found ourselves squashed in with at least twenty other passengers, with two chickens under my seat! We soon reached the destination, paid appropriately 500/-(20p), and continued on foot to our pre-arranged lift to Kampala, the capital city. The streets of Kampala were different to elsewhere in Uganda. There were disabled people and lepers begging, but these beggars were dressed as the rich people in the rural areas were.

Thursday 6th September.

All five of us squashed into a three-man tent; which was not a bad nights' sleep, considering the lack of space. I awoke to see the sun rise through the open tent door; pinks, oranges and reds – breathtaking. After making use of the available showering facilities, we settled down to read about our next destination: the Ssesse Islands. In search of some breakfast, we wandered down the road to a local shop and bought every single samosa they had – all twelve of them. This breakfast, supplemented with bananas and chapattis, enabled us to enjoy a relaxed morning, the highlight of which was being visited by the monkeys.

The bus station was a place of utter chaos and confusion, full of people trying to sell us things and other people desperate to take us somewhere. The bus was not leaving until it was full, so we decided upon a 'special-hire mutato'. A marching band randomly passed heralding the opening of a new company and eventually, after much bartering, we all climbed aboard our chosen mutato and we were off.

Almost immediately, we stopped at a petrol station and typically the driver the driver began to try his luck. He tried to renegotiate the price *and* destination – no way. We did not budge over the price, but ended up having to find a different mutato to get to the port in Musaka. During this journey, we stopped at the equator and took the obligatory photographs as well as buying a musungu-priced watermelon, which was highly welcome. Before long we arrived at Nayemba, paid the mutato driver, and another mutato quickly appeared to take us on the second step of our journey. This involved an hour's wait before we even set off for the port. We were parked by the side of a street, next to various shops including butchers with bits of gut and intestine hanging up outside! During this time we decided that a loo break was needed so we asked the mutato conductor and he led us off into the back streets where for 200/- we were taken through narrow little alleyways, past people cooking lunch and children playing, to a surprisingly decent pit latrine.

By 16:00 we had arrived at the port and everybody was loaded onto the ferry. A rather wobbly rode took us to the island. On arrival at the campsite we were met by Matilda, who runs it, and shown our wooden cabin dorms. Once settled in, we started to explore our new surroundings. It was early evening and the sun was setting. A small private beach with white sand and framed with tropical looking trees and bushes – idyllic! Our beds were literally 50m from the beach with the lake gently lapping on the shore.

Friday 7th September.
Woke up to sun, sand and sea (well, lake). Chapatti rolls for breakfast, but not before an early morning swim. The water is lovely and warm, rather shallow, but still refreshing. This period of relaxation is the perfect way with which to end our Ugandan experience!

At breakfast we met Money, a velvet monkey who had been abducted from the wild at six weeks old and then rescued by Matilda who was hoping he would re-discover the wild when he is scheduled to want a wife at approximately sixteen months old. Money appears to have already made a few monkey friends, but still hangs around the campsite.

Mid-morning and I decided to go in search of some lunch. A neighbouring village produced some bananas and biscuits. It felt very strange wandering into a village consisting of simple mud huts, but the villagers were totally friendly and did not seem to think our presence at all unusual. This island, Kalangala, has a fair amount of musungu tourists, but still has the appearance of being off the beaten track, which is great. After a few more swims, some volleyball etc, the sky clouded over and huge rumbles of thunder signified the beginning of a downpour. I am now sitting under a shelter looking out at the storm. The lake had become shrouded in mist and the other side of the bay is barely visible, reminiscent of the Lady of the Lake.

Saturday 8th September.
Reality set in today and we realised that, inevitably, our funds were decidedly low. The result of this was our decision to experiment with hand-made chapattis. Once the fire was roaring, we set about mixing the flour with some warm water in order to make some suitable dough. We soon attracted the attention of Matilda and Tyson who were keen to give a helping hand but quickly started laughing because we had been sold the wrong flour – maize instead of wheat flour; but at least we had the right ingredients for posho, oh no!

Once swapped, the dough began to take a far more chapatti-like form and was soon ready to fry. It was at around this time that we met Money the cheeky monkey who then stole some of our dough. After hours of slaving around the fire, and several chapattis later, we decided to take a break and go for a refreshing dip in the lake. The weather had definitely taken a turn for the better and we were able to enjoy an afternoon roasting , as well as getting to know the monkeys better!

By late afternoon we had built up the fire again in preparation for our supper of chapattis and sardines. We contemplated cooking the 'huge' fish we had caught earlier, but decided chapattis would do us fine. The evening (our last on the island) soon passed by, sitting around the fire, although not before a stunning sunset and a true African appreciation moment.

Monday 10th September.

After packing away our kit for the final time, we jumped on a *mutatu* and headed for the centre of Kampala. My first priority was breakfast, but when we approached a fruit stall we realised that the prices were extortionate, so we walked away. Passing at the time was a small woman with a basket of bananas on her head – so we paid her the appropriate price and quickly demolished a bunch. We suddenly realised however, that she could just have been a member of the public passing by and we had just bought her personal shopping. However, she seemed happy enough and probably made a profit! Our journey to the airport took us past a passion fruit stall and a place that sold wooden stools – vital, last minute purchases. After nearly a month, our Ugandan experience has finally come to an end.

"Experience is not what happens to you. It is what you do with what happens to you."
Aldous Huxley

"A rattlesnake that doesn't bite teaches you nothing."
Jessamyn West

LADYSMITH IN HARMONY
Elizabeth Kalfsbeek

A review from Cape Town of the South African band, Ladysmith Black Mambazo's album, In Harmony

Recording South Africa's National Sports Anthem, made popular by the Rugby World Cup, is a far cry from Saturday night amateur singing competitions. Such has been the success of the South African ensemble, Ladysmith Black Mambazo.

Mambazo's 1999 *In Harmony* album depicts the *isicathamiya* music genre, made popular as men migrated away from home seeking wage labour. Leaving their families behind, migrant laborers had only each other for company. Each Saturday night they would congregate in male, acapella choirs. The sessions became an efficient way for ordinary people to sing about everyday types of things in order to blow off steam before their day of rest.

The new music genre has been influenced by external groups introducing new musical forms, with which the subordinate group twists in order to fit their own musical values and aesthetics. Such factors include Christian hymns learned in British and Dutch missionary schools, which African-American missionaries introduced African-American spirituals.

The congregations began competing for small monetary prizes, or food, such as perhaps a goat. Singing turned into choreographed dancing as well, with elements of ballroom and tap, influenced in part by American films. African-American minstrel and vaudeville types toured South Africa, which similarly influenced the performers. A type of "ragtime" dance was created, given the Zulu name *ukaraka*. Mambazo won so many of the Saturday night competitions that people refused to contend against them. It was the *Graceland* album with Paul Simon that gained them international recognition.

Topics of *isicathamiya* are not separate from activities of daily life. The rhythmic pulse is soothing. The beat alters a person's perception of time so that the day seems to go faster. The song *Nomathemba*, for example, is about a man who begs for his wife back. This song is also bandleader Joseph Shabalala's first composition, written in 1965.

Similarly, *Our Father we are here*, *Wake up Jonah let us pray*, and *The path is clear*, are songs about aspects of Christian life. *Hello my baby* and *Children of the temple* are songs about family life and values.

Beyond their characteristic topical themes, Mambazo's songs sound as though the choir voices have blended into one. Their harmonies are open sounds, often with a raspy, breathy tone quality of voice. There is little separation of vocal notes, and instead a great deal of sliding between the pitches. The "call and response" theme is also prevalent. This is especially noticeable in the traditional Zulu song, *Abezizwe*, and in the South African song *Shosholoza*, now the National Sports Anthem.

Audiences will surely recognize *Mbube*, which is the established African rendering of *Wimoweh*, also known to the West as *The Lion Sleeps Tonight*. Similarly, Des'ree's contribution to Bill Withers's hit *Ain't No Sunshine*, will be embraced for it's funky beat. *Amazing Grace* is a special treat, arranged with the help of Paul Simon.

The Zulus believe that performers, such as Mambazo, by virtue of directing the flow of energy through movement and words are considered privileged in the handling of the power and flow of destiny. The compilation of songs on *In Harmony* may make the audience feel the same way.

As a Shona native once put it, "Africa may have been colonized by Europe, her people oppressed and mistreated, but Africa conquered the entire world musically."

"If a man does not keep pace with his companions, perhaps it is because he hears a different drummer. Let him step to the music which he hears, however measured or far away."
Henry David Thoreau

THE RICKSHAW
Danny Arkus

Bangladesh isn't really what you would call a normal holidaying destination, so when the strange occurs it is not that atypical.

"Come on. Get up!" Dad shouted as I struggled to open my eyes. I was still jet-lagged and tired after the long journey from New York. He added in his usual neurotic fashion

"We have to be at the airport in four hours, and we don't want to miss the plane!"

We've missed planes before, but never because we were late to the airport. I struggled out of bed and blurted the usual inaudible obscenities at my father before I clumsily made my way to the shower.

"I'm going to go and have some breakfast, as it's included," my Dad said. God forbid that he ever miss a free meal!

"Ok, I might see you down there," I bellowed from my nice hot shower, my equivalent to a cup of coffee. The bathroom wasn't too nice, and there was an overpowering odour of damp and humidity. But nonetheless I had my shower.

Of course, five minutes into my lovely shower, the hot water in the Anderson boiler ran out. My blasted father had used up all of the bloody water! I'd have to wash all the soap off with cold water.

I walked downstairs to the so-called dinning room, which also smelled of damp and humidity. The whole country in fact was oppressively humid, as the Monsoons had still not arrived. In the dinning room my Dad was sipping coffee from a once white cup that had been stained brown through over-use and not enough washing. His glasses were perched on the end of his nose and he smiled as he saw me walk in.

"You'll never guess what's happened today!"

"What?" I replied emotionally drained.

"The taxis have gone on strike. Aren't you glad that we got up early now?" My Dad was clearly very happy about his decision.

"Yeah, I'm delighted, what are we going to do now, walk to the airport?"

"No, the waiter has informed me that we can take a rickshaw as it isn't that far away." My spirits plummeted; these rickshaws were nothing more than over-glorified tricycles with a covering to shield the sun.

"Wonderful! You do realize that we have suitcases?"

"How the hell do you intend to fit us and the suitcase onto the rickshaw?"

"I suppose that we'll have to take two," my Dad answered.

The hotel flagged two down, and I got in one with my suitcase, and my Dad in the other with his. We made our way onto the main road, as cars zipped by us. The airport was about twenty minutes away by rickshaw. I settled back and saw the endless row of flimsy, corrugated tin-roofed houses that appeared to have just exploded out of the centre of the city. Looked around, and then back. . .

"What are you doing?" I exclaimed as I saw my Dad waving with a cupped hand, just as the Queen would.

"I remember the days of the raj!" he said successfully putting on a posh accent...I suppose his days at Oxford did serve a purpose after all.

"Oh god dad, you really do need help."

Five minutes later, the airport came into view; I glanced at my watch and saw that we were still three hours early!

"It's only when we truly know and understand that we have a limited time on Earth—and that we have no way of knowing when our time is up, that we begin to live each day to the fullest, as if it were the only one we had."
Elizabeth Kubler-Ross

LOITERING MALES AND EXCESS BAGGAGE
Vivien Leadbitter

'Madam, you cannot carry 18 kilograms of hand luggage!'

I gulped, smiled and mumbled that I'd be back. As per usual in India, a loitering male felt it his right and proper duty to aid me in my moment of distress. Well, I say 'moment' but actually I was having considerable difficulties with Airport Security. A year living under the influence of Bollywood films and 'Ahmed baby-milk' in my tea had obviously gone to my head - I'd left every imaginable electrical and battery-powered item that I owned in my bulging suitcase. Having spent a half-hour jumping on it the night before (no exaggeration), it was with consternation that I rooted around for all of those 'suspicious objects' that lit up so brightly on the screen. My panic dissipated somewhat at the sight of four security men trying in vain to close the case again.

Having acclimatised myself to the weather I was dressed in a sari and therefore, like any respectable Indian girl, unsuited to jumping around like the mini-skirted girls of Bollywood. Instead, the rest of the departing passengers and I were treated to the sight of four grown men tackling my suitcase as if it were a dangerous beast. Once closed and 'approved', my case was returned to me so that I could walk with it to the other side of the check-in hall. I can only assume that this was to give me one last opportunity to insert some dangerous object before the case was taken from me.

Back to the overweight luggage dilemma. After extracting a few tacky souvenirs and leaving many more inside - with loitering male at my heels - I loaded my bags onto the scale once more. Rapidly calculating excess baggage in rupees, I nodded encouragingly to the bored stewardess. Then the incredible occurred: having laboriously stamped and stickered my documents, the stewardess thoughtlessly pressed the little red button and my forty odd kilograms of luggage trundled onto the conveyor belt. Glancing at the digital scales a fraction too late, she looked up for assurance from (no, not the inept foreign girl in the sari) but the loitering male. He nodded authoritatively and she ushered me onwards. Never again would I scorn the institution of the loitering male.

You might think that this would be the end of my tale. Surely this is the part where I slip snugly into the air-conditioned cabin and amuse myself for hours with in-flight magazines and those oh-so-cute packets of wet wipes and toothpicks. Not so—it must be remembered that I was leaving New Delhi, not New York. Indeed, where would the fun be if one could glide effortlessly through the Departure Lounge, only to spend hours meandering through aisles of Swiss chocolate before settling for a Kit-Kat and a bottle of water?

You would only realise at the front of a long and impatient queue that your boarding pass was buried in the bottom of your bag underneath the change of undies that your mother always made you pack. ('What if there's bad weather, or an air-traffic controller strike, or someone goes into labour en route and the plane has to land in Addis Ababa for a night? Indeed!)

Instead I reach the Customs Desk, swinging my 18 kgs of hand luggage jauntily to ward off anyone searching out excess baggage fraudsters. My passport is dutifully laid down and my all-correct visa displayed. I proudly lay out the tax forms that took me a long frustrating day in Delhi to obtain. 'How much money did you bring into the country?', 'How much did you spend?' I had scrupulously run through every mango and grain of rice that I had ever bought before flinging out a random figure that sounded theoretically possible. From office to office I had traipsed to get the 'correct' stamps and signatures. Colonial bureaucracy has quite a large legacy to answer for.

'Ah, but where is your police form?'

'Police form?' I mumbled, knowing full well that I did not have one because a friend had tried, only to have the provincial police on her doorstep, frightening the life out of her host family. They had told her she hadn't needed to report to the police, after ignoring her valid visa and demanding to know why she was in the country.

I decided not to relate this detail to the languidly amused officer in front of me. I could see him smiling at the stupidity of this young, foreign girl with a sari on. Then to my surprise, there appeared not a loitering male but a knight in shining armour—or rather in the smart uniform of the Customs Service who swooped in to save the day. The fellow officer had seen my plight and was now arguing my case in Hindu. By now I understood the gist of conversations and I revelled at his turns of phrase and his nods and gestures. I, of course, stood demurely smiling. Eventually I discovered that I was to be allowed through, but not now, in a half-hour when his 'friend' would let me pass. One does not question the logic of a Customs Officer so I fled to a distant corner where I could people-watch and relieve my shoulder of its 18 kg burden. After 20 minutes, the officer approached me.

'Why are you still here?' he laughed. 'You can go through!'

As I say, never question the logic of someone who is clearly on a quest to 'save face'. I went through with only a minor hiccup in which my stereo batteries were confiscated to be returned 'at the end of the flight'. Because I planned to stop in Dubai to visit a friend, I gave up all hope of seeing them again and stepped into the air-conditioned cabin, smiling as I think of my 58 kgs of luggage and the relative organisation of home. I will perhaps miss those loitering males. Perhaps...

CRUEL PUNISHMENT
Rachel Kondo

A story regarding not a destination but the moments just prior.

Sitting silently and profoundly at Gate 120 of the Los Angeles Airport, I felt a heaviness in having left my home, Maui, the day before to begin my trek half way around the world to my new home in Scotland. Knowing that life for me as I've always known it was to take such a dramatic turn, I became fearful that I wouldn't recognize what has always been and, in the middle of this thought, I looked up and slightly left to find a gentleman steadily meet my eye. Hmmm. Slightly uncomfortable. But I was quite amazed at the same time...amazed that he could still see in his geriatric condition. It was only unnerving when I realized that I was his visual selection for the evening. "Ladies and Gentlemen, we are now boarding rows 40-50" (the most unfavourable seating next to the toilets, she should have added). As our consolation prize, we were on the plane first. I exhaled, said good-bye to American soil and proceeded to seat 48K, where my story really begins.

The only point in time when drinking water on a consistent basis is a poor decision is when you have the window seat. The only thing worse is when the gentleman sitting next to you, like a big boulder with blinders, may be dead or just sleeping. I, too, attempted to sleep; however, whenever the curtain of my lids fell, the feeling of my bladder bag tearing from the pressure within continued on. I thought it a clever plan to glance in the boulder's direction every four seconds for several hours and finally caught him checking his watch, meaning he was alive and, please God, awake. I must have startled him with how fast my hand snapped to tap his shoulder, ever-so-gently, so as to appear absolutely composed with five litres of built-up urine threatening to flood my body chamber and drain through my ears and nostrils. Well, I managed to get to the bathroom, finally, which thanks to choice seating was a mere three steps away. Ahhhhhhhhhhh.

Returning to my row, I noticed, once again how my neighbour, Mr. Narcoleptic, had to my ultimate surprise, fallen back asleep. Now where falling asleep may not have been intentional or possibly even helped, realigning blinders over his eyes was down right cruel. Anticipating another four hours of waiting for him to check his watch, I stood absolutely still over him and squinted my eyes so as to narrow the stream of laser I imagined my eyeballs to emit and penetrate his blinders, and hopefully brain. And just when it seemed that laser-eyes weren't the solution of the day, the problem solved itself: the passenger directly behind me began kicking the headrest of the sleeping man with his extended leg and foot. I suppose it worked; the man

awoke and looked at me as one would a crazed seat-kicker. I just sort of gig-
gled, I think. I thanked him politely and then quickly shuffled into my seat. I
remembered the gentleman behind me who oh-so-kindly went out of his way
to assist (could that be the word?) me in the difficult process of sitting down.
So I turned to thank him, and yes, it was him: elderly man who should either
number one, not be able to see or number two, not have lust in his eyes for a
girl sixty-five years his junior. He began speaking to me in a language unfamiliar and I again managed a quick giggle and even quicker turn around to
sit back down.

A few seconds pass and I am faced with a decision: Moulin Rouge
soundtrack, Alfred Hitchcock movie, Bird by Bird (by Anne Lamot; it's excellent, by-the-way), or, sensing my indecision and with the wisdom of many,
MANY years, my friend behind decided for me: I was going to sleep. "Young
Ameri-kan...must sleep." He then tucked his pillow, along with my own that
he reached over and grabbed, against the window. Holding the two pillows
up with his right hand, he buffeted his arrangement with his airplane blanket. "Oh, I'm to sleep, I suppose," I say, not knowing what else to do and
feeling a bit strange to have him breathing overhead. "Young Ameri-
kan.....sleep......better," rambled his thick accent, slurred with intoxication.
Again, there was no time for me to think whether or not I'd like to sleep;
decisions were being made for me. Working like a man with a mission, the
man continued to hold up the arrangement with his right hand and then,
noticing my hesitation, used his left to slam my head up against the little bed
he had made for me.

"SLEEP!"

Um. I wondered silently if this was against some sort of law. I then
began to wonder how our legal system would translate for him and how the
International Court of Justice might handle this one and would the UN need
to get involved...I didn't want to sleep. Surely that was not a crime.

But oh, it was. I had slowly slid from the arrangement of pillows and
blankets when my ever-so-attentive friend (whom I'm hoping was attentive
for certain paternal reasons and not pelvic) again took matters into his own
hands, well my head in his hand, and slammed it back into his set-up. Okay,
I had had enough. I remained at the arrangement for a minute or two, thinking what I should do, and then it came to me: I would sit up. Hawk-eyes
from behind of course noticed my insurrection. Understanding exactly how
ungrateful I was (after all his sacrifice and service, really, I should be in a
coma), he viciously and spitefully snapped his pillow away..........then my
pillow..........then his blanket..........and finally *my* blanket (which had never
even been involved in the first place).

Cruel, cruel punishment.

MEETING WITH MAO
Simon Moriarty

What – where – is the *real* China? The China of rickshaws and rice-fields, dragons and firecrackers? The China of myth and history? The answer, it seems, is nowhere. It is slowly sinking out of sight, overwhelmed by technology and pollution, disease, war and poverty. The China I experienced is slowly but surely emerging after decades of turbulence, concealed from Western eyes: a sleeping giant that will one day surely find its feet.

There is no real China, for no one essence encapsulates everything about a country. If stereotype and myth were all a country had; if everything was easily digestible in bite-size portions of clichés and tourist hotspots, the world would be a much poorer place. Of course, stereotype has its place, but when we first looked into going to the Far East, there was really very little that anyone could tell us.

'It'll be cold… freezing… colder than anything you've ever experienced.' (It wasn't. It was sunny and warm.) 'Everything is ridiculously cheap. You don't need to take that much money.' (I ran out of cash a couple of days before coming home, and it was only thanks to Mr Visa that I could afford the mandatory departure tax at the airport.) But the most consistent response was, 'China? Wow. I mean, *China*? Wow!' And that much, and more, was true. China? Wow.

Beijing is a strange and contradictory sort of place. On one hand, it is the ideal place from which to start a trip around China. It is the capital, after all, a great sprawling area half the size of Belgium. On the other hand, it is the capital, a great sprawling area half the size of Belgium. It is daunting and massive and dirty. Pollution is a huge problem in China, and Beijing maintains a stench of sewage and smoke. There are cars everywhere - even driving on the pavement - and crossing any road at any time is always a challenge. Still, Beijing is at least a headfirst introduction to so exotic a place: not quite sink-or-swim, but I did feel like I was treading water a few times.

The first day was gentle enough, though. The Embassy Area of Beijing is beautifully well kept and ordered, mainly because there are lots of men with rifles strolling around, and the occasional blacked-out limousine cruising past. It is also strangely quiet, because most of the roads around this section of town are open to official vehicles only. Around this area I encountered the fewest Chinese people, only Embassy workers and their families. It was a strange introduction to the city, because it gave the appearance of there being more Westerners around than there actually were. So, during the first day anyway, the enormous feeling of self-consciousness that nearly overwhelmed me by the end of the trip had not yet started to grow.

It was in Tiananman Square the next morning that I suddenly realised how big this place is, not just in terms of size, but population. It is a world away from anything I am used to. In the dawn half-light, the two white faces that joined the crowd watching the changing of the guard were noticeable enough. People turned and stared, or pointed, or nudged their children. One woman even tried to stop her little girl crying by pointing us out and laughing. It didn't work.

Tiananman Square itself is smaller than it looks on the television (isn't everything?) but it is still an impressive, eerie place. Despite all the people, it retains an air of stillness. Perhaps the presence of Chairman Mao's giant portrait staring down from the gateway to the Forbidden City is enough to keep people under control. Maybe it is the fact that his body lies in the centre of the Square, under a glass case and armed protection, a reminder of the power the chain-smoking dwarf had over the people of China. Or perhaps it is the fact that there are soldiers all over the square, a potent echo of the massacre that took place here, and is for many in the West the only experience of China they have had: the tanks rolling past students waving pamphlets and plastic bags is one of the most memorable news images of the Eighties.

Incidentally, we went to see Mao's body. He (is? was?) very small, and apparently the bottom half of his body is covered with a flag because they messed up the embalming process and he is rotting away from the feet upwards. And on the way out of the Mausoleum, in a tasteful gesture of solidarity with their former leader, the vendors sell Mao Cigarettes, in deference to his forty-a-day habit.

Nowhere in Beijing is the past more powerfully evoked than in the Forbidden City. The untouched temples and chambers where the Emperors, Dowagers and Eunuchs held power away from the *hoi polloi* are remarkably pristine and well kept. The vastness of the city within the city is even more telling because there are perhaps hundreds of buildings that are still not open to the public. It really is an amazing place. That effect is spoiled slightly by the audio commentary, which features Roger Moore and the most obviously uninterested, take-the-money-and-run approach to tourist information imaginable. Still, if you can stomach the sardonic tones of an actor more famed for his eyebrows than any thespian tendencies, there is a lot to gain from a trip to the Forbidden City. As a historical relic it is near-perfect, but it also gives a better understanding of the schizophrenic nature of China, and the fractured past that it has suffered. Like the Forbidden City itself, it is only fragments that can be seen.

Behind the Forbidden City lies the artificial Prospect Hill, famous for its giant Buddha and the views of the city. Despite the smog – and there is actually a straight line that divides blue sky and grey sky – the views were spectacular, showing the symmetry of the city and the size of Tiananman Square, not fully appreciated from street level. The Buddha sits at the top and gazes serenely down over the view, probably regretting the fact that there used to be several more Buddhas just like him dotted round the hill, but the Allies stole them all in 1900. No one seems entirely sure where these Buddhas are now, but they're not exactly easy to keep hidden. Maybe it's a conspiracy. Or the French.

The next day brought more spectacular views, this time at the Old Summer Palace where the Dowager Empresses used to spend their holidays. Surrounding a magnificent lake, the palace consists of several buildings hiding in the trees on the shore. The lake was frozen over, but the sun was shining, giving the whole place a very still feel. The buildings were similar to those in the Forbidden City with wooden beams and pillars, pointed roofs with intricate carvings of dragons and animals hidden in the gables. The faded reds, yellows and greens blended with the brittle trees and shrubs. This was the China of postcards and books. It was also the China of souvenir stalls. Tourism is a growing business here, and while it was nowhere near as bad as, say, Florence or Bangkok, there are signs that in the next few years places like the palace will be overrun by people selling miniature Buddha statues and butterfly kites. The vendors here are more pushy than their counterparts in developed countries, mainly because they are desperate for the tourist dollar but also because it is in the Chinese nature to be quite in-your-face, unafraid to actually grab hold of tourists and foist what is, unsurprisingly, cheap tat on them. I felt uncomfortable dealing with the vendors. They felt I was a rich Westerner, and I was torn between feeling sorry for them because they were so poor and not wanting to part with my money for a useless piece of crap that neither I, nor anyone back home, would want or use. The basic fact is that most tourists are not as rich as the people targeting them think, and the Chinese people are much poorer than most people realise. It's a tricky situation, and one that doesn't seem easy to avoid.

Luckily, the only vendors on Fragrance Hill were selling drinks. The hill is 520 metres high, and quite steep in parts, but the views of nearby Beijing are well worth it. Again we were the only white faces to be seen, but conversely, the vendors here didn't seem as interested in us. Other people on the hill were, though, and if you will forgive the Sherlock Holmesque detour, a pattern began to emerge. It seemed that children were nonplussed by our presence, and only if they felt brave enough in groups did they point or say anything. People our own age, students on the whole, were more interested in us for the fact that we spoke English. Although this also meant they could manipulate us more easily (or try) it seemed they had a genuine interest in the language as an escape route from poverty. In Shanghai, two students approached us asking if they could practice their English skills. It turned out they wanted to take us to an exhibition where they could try and sell us some of their paintings. The *same* happened in the Forbidden City; the *same* uncomfortable feeling of not wanting to offend people but also not wanting to be ripped off.

It was the older Chinese people who always seemed surprised at our presence, and not always in a particularly welcoming way. Walking down the street in any of the three cities we visited meant walking against a sea of stares. At first this was kind of exciting and not too unpleasant, but by the end of a fortnight it was becoming nearly unbearable. Was it resentment? Fear? It was hard to tell. The Chinese remember a time only too recently when anything that went against the set norm was punished and eradicated. As Westerners, we were walking embodiments of everything inaccessible to the Chinese. We had health, good clothes, shiny guidebooks and passports that allow us free passage throughout most of the world. Most of all, we had the money for a flight to China in the first place, and the money to spend on restaurants and taxis and buses and tourist attractions. It would have been naïve to assume that we would be accepted with open arms in every area of life: we weren't. We were strangers in this country, and we never forgot that. Don't get me wrong, I'm not trying to paint China as a land of unfriendly mercenaries, only after the cash tourists have to offer, because it is not. Far from it.

In a country where the military are omnipresent, where slums sit side by side with gleaming high-rises and where European-style architecture sits on the banks of polluted rivers carrying flat boats loaded with bamboo, there is no easy way of defining China. This country is like a Chinese box: peel back layer after layer to reveal something different beneath the surface: some things are expected, some are not. There is no way of understanding how beautiful the Great Wall is until you have actually walked along its uneven steps in blazing sunshine, with nothing around for miles except rolling hills and steep ravines. There is no way to describe exactly what kind of city Shanghai is without being able to walk along its crowded streets, looking up at the neon street signs, smelling the aromas of cooking sweetmeats and bread. But if this sleeping giant does manage to wake itself, shake off the cobwebs and the hangover of its history and Western perception, will this be a good thing? The unspoiled sights, the Terracotta Warriors, the Great Wall at Samutai, the snow-capped peaks and rolling greens of the vast countryside will become tarnished by tourist boots. For now, China and its people are an enigma. As far-flung destinations go, it is difficult to imagine somewhere so schizophrenic – so beautiful and dirty, so poor and rich at the same time. It was certainly an experience unlike any other.

TRAVELLING YOUNG: 1976-2001
Victoria Quinn

Southampton
Judith, pinched and white, with one long plait
That tickled her scabbed knees, and red-haired Jane
Whose freckles danced like motes of dust
Caught in the sun,
Seized me, dragged me laughing through the door
And rolled me in sweet drifts of cherry-blossom.
Under the weight of gym-slips and brown shoes,
I knew my place was here, patch-kneed
With scabs and sellotape.
Here, with the smell of mince and linseed oil,
The busy hush of church-school classes.
All this I cupped in my straw boater
That last summer.

FIJI

Viti Levu
Beside my cool, grey beliefs I set the cup
Of chili-liquid kava root
Washed in yaqona bowls by numb-eyed men
Wrapped tight in leaves;
The fragrant, gory glory of the Hindu temples;
Ganesh, Shiva, Kali of the skulls.
Each night I hear the piercing whine
Of me-engorged mosquitos trapped
In white, suspended nets;
A crunch
Of feral dogs; dark screeching and
The liquid pulse of rain upon pandanus.
We live in tabu lands. They are veined
With slick stone chutes; the rich
Black green of mango trees; spiked breadfruit;
Frangipani; guava; sour-mouthed
Lipstick plants and jangles of lantana.
On high days, holy days, I walk the wire.
Drawn behind my father with his bag
Of long collecting spoons and empty jars,

I pace the black-etched brittle stars
And knobbled limpets. We scoop
Mantled cowries; polished, lethal, dart-tipped cones.
Once, among the rippling Spanish Dancers,
I tripped and plunged into a shallow pool
Alive with tiny, gem-bright fins and blue-lipped clams.
Face down among the puffing cuttlefish
I burned the tips off both my ears
I was so lost.

The Rongovoka's Last Voyage
The morning we caught the manta ray
The sky turned from blue to black
And the crew got down on their knees to pray
When the halyards all went slack.
The Captain saw that the sea'd gone still
So his heart was in his mouth,
But he'd broken a contract once before -
This time he kept on south.
On board was a man who could see him dead
Or locked up in an island goal;
A woman too - that could mean no good -
He was damned if he didn't sail.
When the sun went down the night came alive
In a flicker of light and sound.
Waves started to knock on the rusted prow:
It was too late to turn around.
By now, the sea was running high
And the crew on the boats had hid.
He grasped the wheel between callused hands
Then commended himself to God.
Down below decks in the stagnant dark
His passengers hauled on their door.
It was welded shut by the drumming tide;
It was just for one moment clear.
As the man fell through on the salt-scrubbed planks,
Leaving his wife feeling ill,
He heard a thunderous crash, looked up,
Saw the focsle crumpled like silk.
He fought his way to the Captain's side,
'There's an island ahead,' he gasped.

'Can't we alter course and shelter there?'
'We can, sir, now you've asked.'
The two men hung on the buckling wheel
Till they turned the ship slow right.
By the break of day they had landed safe,
Now the passenger feared for his wife.
'We should never have sailed with a woman aboard,'
Cried the Boson that afternoon.
'All know it's bad luck. We must leave her behind
If we're saved. Men, you know that it's true.'
'It's not my poor wife that is really to blame,'
The passenger, angry, replied.
'It's the manta ray that the Ship's Boy caught.
That gave birth on the deck as it died.
'Remember how we'd said to put it back,
But you chopped it up live, just for fun.
Though the albatross haunts my northern seas,
It's the manta here, old son.'
Three weeks they were stranded, out there, alone,
Then a tramp steamer saw their mast.
They rescued the passengers, Captain and crew -
There was only the Boson lost.

Armitage Shanks
In the middle of the rustling,
Razor-edged bamboo
Was a toilet bowl.
It was quite isolate.
Pale, hard and cool
And self-contained.
Inside, ferns, coiled tight
As watch-springs or
Kiss-curls of fine black wire.
Through the hot, flat planes of light,
The drowning, swooning blue
Of morning glory,
Flies a white, imperial flag
Before the green, the serried ranks:
Armitage. Shanks.

A HORROR TRIP HOME
Lisanne Ebert

St. Andrews on a lovely Wednesday morning just before Easter. It's 8:50 a.m. I'm about to board a bus toward Edinburgh – the Mecca for all Scottish students. Athough I haven't slept much recently due to weeks of relentless, hard work, I'm in an extremely good mood. The night before I couldn't sleep at all, since I was so excited about returning home to Munich, not to mention the attractive prospect of a subsequent visit to marvellous Italy. The birds are singing – so am I.

There is a long queue; everybody wants to get out of St Andrews. The bus driver – a sleazy young man with slimy black hair styled *'a la Hitlerjugend'* is rather mal-humoured. He seems very annoyed by the fact that it takes me a few minutes to load my three suitcases onto the bus, as no one is polite enough to give me a hand.

I buy a ticket, which proves to be more of a hassle: there are only student discounts to Edinburgh, so if I get off at Glenrothes (where I want to do some shopping), I have to pay *twice* the amount for half the distance!

The dilemma is forcibly solved after ten kilometres anyhow. I am kicked off the bus in the middle of the road because I converse loudly with fellow passengers, and unconsciously say 'f**k' or 'f**king' in the middle of the sentence. I have to admit, this is not a very nice habit of mine. However, I acquired my English skills in the United States, where 'fuck' is an inevitable, integral part of everyday vocabulary, just as 'mingin' or 'bloody' are part of the strange assortment of the non-intelligible speech of the Scots.

Fortunately, a young woman that followed the bus is more than willing to take me to the next town, Kirkcaldy, in her car. I arrive at the bus station just in time to board the same bus I started off with in St Andrews. At this point, the bus driver is going mad and calls the police to say he is not willing to continue driving the bus if I am on board.

The police ask no questions, and legally prohibit my partaking on this merry bus drive. The bus driver, however, is so confused and enraged that he leaves Kirkcaldy without even picking up the waiting passengers. Well, what shall one do on such a lovely morning? Let a bus driver alternate my mood? Definitely not.

So I cross the road where a young guy is smoking away in his car. He is more that willing to take me to Glenrothes, since he does not have a bust schedule either. After having thanked the nice young chap, I proceed to do my shopping in my favourite shop 'Bay,' then arrive at the bus station just in time to catch an *earlier* bus. That's the way life goes: twisted and unfair.

Having checked all my luggage at Edinburgh airport, I'm bored! After such an exciting journey starting in St Andrews, I have now come to realize that I am actually quite exhausted. To make matters better, the seats on GO airlines are extremely uncomfortable and unsuitable for brief airborne snoozes. Nevertheless, I pass out and wake up again at London Stansted.

At this point I am so tired that I can't be bothered to keep my thoughts to myself. Pondering out loud is a wonderfully refreshing and amusing thing, I discovered, especially in such a busy, annoyingly hectic and stressful atmosphere. On this lovely Wednesday before Easter it looks like everyone has the same idea I do – get out of Britain and find the warmth!

Though the British take their queuing business very seriously, I did not feel like joining the mile long lines towards nowhere (especially since I felt a certain bladder weakness). I just sat down on a bench, started talking to children (the only human beings on earth, it seems, to have time and energy to participate in irrelevant, informal conversation), telling them about German Easter bunnies, and complaining about the inefficiency and inadequacy of the airport on such a busy day. I literally felt like an unpaid street clown – though in the eyes of certain other passengers this matter seemed to be of a more serious nature.

The Big Mistake happened just before I was to check my suitcases through to Munich. I felt a sudden, desperate need to run to the toilet. With only three people queuing now, I asked a person sitting next to me to keep an eye on two of my bags for a second.

This sad person must have seriously thought I was hiding weapons or bombs in my suitcases. In any case, the person was gone when I returned. Instead, a cop was standing in front of my luggage. He grabbed my arm in a very un-British, cruel and impolite way and tried to drag me aside. I panicked. Knowing that I needed to check in immediately, I apparently raised my voice to a level inappropriate when dealing with a person in authority. Needless to say, I missed my flight, and had no choice but to spend the night on a sofa at the Stanstead airport.

London at noon. I am in the banking quarter close to Baker Street. I stand at the doorstep of a quaint little pub, after having been given a lift from Liverpool station by an obliging young gentleman on his way to work.

The bar is still empty. I store my entire luggage in one corner and sit down on a sofa to pass out. I'm soon reminded that I should perhaps not sleep in public restaurants. Instead, I take out my laptop and several books and begin fiddling.

Some young business men (solicitors as far as I could gather) enter and approach the bar. I start some conversation with one of them; tell him bits and pieces of my previous day. Since there are no flights until Saturday and I am free all day, he asks me to join him for a quick gym session in the Dome. I take a shower, get changed, and feel a lot better.

I go and have a coffee at a café around the corner run by some very lively Portuguese, where I enjoy a huge slice of chocolate cake with ice cream. Then, I decide that sharing cake is even more fun, so I start offering customers pieces of my cake. People are hesitant. Eating a stranger's cake strikes them as abnormal. Think of all the evil germs and bacteria! This is a particularly welcome excuse, since everybody nowadays seems to be on a diet.

I spend that night in the Savoy Hotel. After my troublesome travelling experiences I am not feeling too well. My behaviour, based on the lethal concoction of lack of sleep, blatant sarcasm, and unpleasant encounters with the impolite bus driver, must seem quite strange to the outer world, while I am still living in my own world.

It turns out that the bad film I am trapped in was more serious than I had thought. After complaining about severe back pain the next morning (the inevitable outcome of carrying around three bags for three days, while simultaneously suffering a bladder infection), the Savoy called an ambulance. At first I thought this was all extremely amusing, though when I woke next up in St. Thomas Hospital, drugged with antibiotics, valium and other chemical substances, I felt my body had started to capitulate.

I lost contact with reality, only regaining my senses when I arrived in Munich after my parents had collected me from the hospital. A nightmare indeed, and a lesson for life. Don't play if you don't want to be played around with! Well, at least not on Scottish buses, and at London airports.

AN ITALIAN CAFÉ, COVENT GARDEN
Francesca Troiania

Taking this solitary moment
A bleak anticipation
Of time unoccurring.
Like when you're waiting
But doing other things –
Reading a paper looking
For a chance, an
Inspiration, a line that will
Clarify your Freedom,
But it is only the light wood table
...The voices...
The taste of buds from
Coffee well-brewed.
It doesn't make sense
After cigarette
Article on a black
Poet that forged his
London Identity
And discovered who He was
Through the finding of a half brother, long-lost
And then
      "I shall have an Irish
      Coffee, please,"
Is voiced loudly by the
Guy at the table in front,
Doesn't he know he's supposed to have
Italian coffee in an Italian place?
A bumping door,

Japanese; laughing, young
People in the corner
Shaking sugar-straws
Before they are
Ripped and opened and sssss'd
Into the coffee.
So in this moment
That keeps passing
Sitting in my own
Loud silence
I scream
Because I must go on,
Follow the direction
I'm grooved into,
That I know.

The poetry of motion! The real way to travel! The only way to travel! Here today-in next week tomorrow! Villages skipped, towns and cities jumped- always somebody else's horizon!
Kenneth Grahame, The Wind in the Willows.

A TRIP TO THE TROPICS
A A Guilherme

After spending three years in Britain, I decided that this was the proper time to go back home and spend a whole month under true sunshine. This time I took a British friend to the country where I was born and brought up and was aware that I was going to introduce a completely different way of life to him.

Although of Italian origin, I was born and raised in Sao Paulo, Brazil, and that is where we were heading. The overhead speakers at the airport lounge announced that boarding was due to begin. I love take-offs and landings but absolutely hate anything in between, especially if the 'in-between' is twelve hours long and a sleepless nightmare. We arrived at *Cumbica*, Sao Paulo's international airport, forty-five minutes early, and I thought, this is fantastic! *Spoke too soon*. The airport was understaffed and we therefore had to wait for an hour and fifteen minutes for our luggage. Typically Brazilian: no rush, take it easy.

We met my family, introduced my friend and headed home. In between the airport and my parent's house, three things were very noticeable: graffiti, potholes and shanty-towns, though not necessarily in that order. Some things never change. My British friend was mortified, surprised and speechless.

After a week in Sao Paulo you discover there is not much to see, really; unless you are interested in skyscrapers, sixties architecture, a lack of trees, and large shopping centres. Therefore, we decided to travel around and headed for the wonderful city of Rio. It has been cleared up; both rubbish and crime have been noticeably reduced these days. Corcovado, Sugarloaf, Ipanema, Copacabana, The Botanical Gardens, and Lapa Arches are absolutely fantastic and extremely beautiful. The most striking thing about Rio is its natural beauty. No city in the world has been built in a more breathtaking setting. Rio for me is paradise on earth.

Our next stop was Salvador. A city in the Northeast of Brazil, which is very popular with the French and Italians. It is a UNESCO monument since it possesses the largest amount of seventeenth and eighteenth century

Portuguese colonial architecture anywhere in the world. The old city is colourful, and teeming with restored villas and innumerable churches replete with gold furnishings, paintings, statues and frescos. Salvador is a real time trip back to colonial Brazil of the seventeenth and eighteenth century. Another treat of the old city is the smell of palm oil, as it seeps into everything because of the sheer number of small stands selling local delicacies cooked in the oil. Also, watch for the folklore dancing shows, which happen at least three times a day and are beautifully free.

The new city is blooming with modern buildings, which where designed by a local architect. But Salvador is more than a contrast between old and new; it also possess a beautiful natural setting. The city was built in the second largest bay in the world, the bay of *All Saints*, and the beaches have palm tress everywhere, not crowded, just clean, sunny and gorgeous. A day trip to a desert island aboard a tall ship is also well worthwhile – try it!

After Salvador it was time to go back to Sao Paulo, say goodbye to the family and friends, and then take our plane back to Britain – the journey back, as you can probably guess, was a twelve-hour long nightmare had while wide awake. We arrived on time, our luggage was unloaded pronto, no problems whatsoever. British style.

ISCHIA PORTA
Irene Caselli

learning to be for myself-
two strata of clouds
and paradise colours
brief impressions
still time to think
to explain to be

---

nude - dublin

song of other moments
movies or
n5 kitchen cleaning

brown tastes of winter
rainy days
with faces now away
-what am i looking for
with this?

try more try more
i can do more - i can be more
or just be myself
if i could find myself

---

dingle

guinness foam on your lips
memories as usual
meaty lips
want to kiss them
fishy maybe
want to eat them
and say goodnight

almost reached
the most westerly place
in europe
the horizon so vast
other skies
the ocean
so quiet so flat
you're so much closer
but still so far

---

spot of light at the horizon
a miracle there
so many dreams
so many thoughts
and energy
and still another huge land
and an ocean to divide us

---

o'flahertys

ice melting in my glass
face tired
like a rock slapped
by the sun, the wind
the sea water
music- fiddles
faces, true faces
and tourist faces
people wondering
what it is i write
-if only i knew

m.'s kitchen, suffolk

long day? not really
not much happened
floated in a space
not mine
felt at home
in this other part
of the world
listened to words stories
and was a good friend
for a day
-but then my thoughts
memories
exploded after
curry and limoncello
-tastes of other moments
did it
or the music
-and now i only
need to go not think
and it has to be a
good book, i suppose

ischia porto

need some kind
of travelling
to feel inspired,
understand how i am,
look at things
from a different
perspective,
and attempt to write poetry

IMPRESSIONS FROM A FRANCOPHILE
Sara Gill

"My automatic images of 'being in France' are initially pictorial: quiet canals lined with trees as regular as comb-teeth[..], dormant vines[..]morning mist[..] working villages with rusting café tables, lunchtime torpor[..]the dusty thud of boules and an all-purpose épicerie[..]."
Julian Barnes, Something to Declare

Mamers

How, then, to describe the ambience of rural small town life in France, which is everything that the clichés suggest, and more?

Mamers, hidden away in the sarthois countryside with only 6,000 inhabitants, is the kind of town that tourists might drive through without taking a second glance. First impressions, however, are often misleading. After only a few months I was totally captivated by the rural charm of this beautiful town, where the days are punctuated by the church bells and the pace of life is slow and relaxed: c'est *la France profonde…* where time poses no obstacles.

Each period of the day in Mamers takes on a different perspective…

At daybreak, the *Mamertins* (those living in Mamers) carry out their morning preparations; shopkeepers, so fiercely proud of their work, sweep away the dust from the shop's entrance; whilst in the cafés, old men sit by the bar, with either a small glass of *calvedos* or a *petit café noir* in hand, and philosophise on the state of France. At the end of the morning, as the hands on the church clock near midday, Mamers springs into life. The townspeople bustle in and out of the *boulangeries* buying their baguettes, the school children rush out onto the streets, on their way home for lunch *en famille* and all this against the background of the church bells ringing, calling people home for lunch.

During the lunch period (12.30-14.30) all the shops and cafés close, and a sense of tranquillity descends upon the town: nothing stirs….

Later, twilight in Mamers, the shop windows illuminated against a backdrop of pink and lilac sky, the old-fashioned lampposts casting eerie shadows across the pavement. The frosty evening air feels clean and refreshing as I make my way across the *Place de la République* and marvel at how pretty it is with its elegant border of trees adorned in their autumn hues. I'm walking along with my baguette (à la française), passing old men with black bérets (oh-so-quintessentially-French) shuffling past me. The houses look welcoming, lights shining out from behind closed shutter and in the distance, the church steeples are silhouetted against the darkening horizon. Hmm, the charm of rural France...

Mad Dogs & Frenchmen
11th November 2001. Paris, Boulevard Saint Germain: homage to Robert Doisneau.

I'm walking along a narrow side street in the direction of the *Jardins de Luxembourg*, I glance through the window of a café as I pass by and see a waiter seated at a table eating his lunch, sitting on the chair opposite him is a large brown bulldog.

The scene, so ridiculous and yet so magnificently Parisian, passes before my eyes in a moment and is stored away in my memory in the format of a classic black and white postcard, à la Robert Doisneau.

1st December 2001. Travelling back from Angers on the *T.G.V.*

My sense of unease heightens, as I shift uncomfortably under the unerring gaze of the traveller sat opposite me on the train: a beautified, coiffed, and manicured prima donna of a white poodle with a snub nose and superior pose.

At the end of my first three months, the realisation dawns upon me: dogs have civil rights in France. *C'est vrai;* they have right of way through shop doors, they are given priority for seat reservations on trains and in restaurants, they are paraded around in chic Chanel shoulder bags by their proud owners. Naturally, every town in France has a poodle parlour. The beauty of the dog community is paramount.

Hmm...Curious, isn't it, given that the French are a people often ridiculed for being reluctant to conform to rules. Yet, the rules concerning the comfort and prestige of dogs, though unwritten, remain observed.

Snapshots
13th October, 2001. Autun, Burgundy.

Imagine: a quaint town with winding cobbled streets, country lanes and cottages with smoking chimneys, boulevards with classy boutiques and bistros, a magnificent central square with elegant 1920's style lampposts, and nearby, gardens where men in bérets play boules. All this is perched upon a hill in full fairytale splendour, the maze of streets that make up the town slope down from its majestic midpoint where the imposing cathedral stands tall, and outside the town, a panorama of forest and lush verdant landscape. Truly idyllic.

5th April 2002. Montpellier.

Montpellier is everything I imagined a city in the South of France to be, and more. Warm sunshine, like honey, pouring down from the sky in abundance onto the pavement cafés in the *Place de la Comédie* below. Here, all the seats are turned to face the centre of the square, the scene in front forming a sort of stage. Thus, the square becomes a point of live theatre in its own right where people sit and watch the world go by.

Wandering around, we find leafy esplanades, à l'espagnole, and parks lined with palm trees, where happy olive skinned children are running around in the sunshine, and chicly dressed business-men, unfazed by the heat, are sitting on benches reading *Le Monde*. These are lazy days, everyone enjoying the sun, there's no rush...

Walking back through the old town, through shady *placettes* with terrace cafés, people clustered at tables enjoying their *aperitif*, one is able to understand the allure of the Provence-Languedoc region.

Afternoon. Sitting by a fountain in the *Place du marché de fleurs*, listening to the now familiar sounds of Montpellier: the chatter and clinking of glasses at pavement cafés, the street musicians playing their melodies, the cascade of water at the fountains, the rumbling of motor bikes and scooters, and dogs barking. The taste of the *Languedoc...*

Evening in the Rue de petit Saint-Jean. Found a Spanish-come-provençal restaurant and enjoyed a simple yet delicious meal sitting outside: *du vin rouge, salade de tomates, moules à la crème d'ail, tarte de pommes* and a *café noir*. The sun is setting, the luminous orange tones of the sky overhead slowly (in accordance with the "no-rush" mentality of the South) dimming. And in the background, the hub-hub of conversation drifting from other tables (the sing-song voices of soupy Southern French), and a man playing a guitar, everyone clapping to the flamenco beat. Even during the nocturnal hours, there is always that distant beat of drums and flamenco music....

16th June, 2002. Biarritz.

A place of paradoxes. The coastline, so natural in its savageness: the force and power of the waves and the rugged rocks, nature untamed...

I stand on the hill by the lighthouse, overlooking the town and the spectacular backdrop of the *Pyrenées* shrouded in a haze of heat.

Then, in contrast, there is another face of Biarritz; a glitzy, almost film-set atmosphere that the town has. Biarritz is showy: women walking around with poodles, the thermal baths, the casino, the boutiques, the windsurfers. It is a place to be seen.

But this showy exterior is only just holding up, walking around one can see signs that Biarritz has passed its heyday. The creepy rambling mansions – mausoleums in their own right, their dark windows looking out on

you like eyes; the dilapidated synagogue round the corner from our apart-
ment, the windows of the adjoining house, where the Rabbi would have lived,
broken, the net curtains swaying in the breeze; the Russian church and the
eerie secrecy of the place and the house next door, dark and desolate. Once I
could have sworn I saw the curtains twitching, even though it was meant to
be empty.

In this sense, Biarritz seems sad and soulless, a place of past glory.

26th June, 2002. Avignon.
Contented moments:

Twilight, the sky darkening: sitting opposite the *Palais des Pape* which
is floodlit against the backdrop of the sky, a spectacular sight. In the background, somewhere in the square, a violin is playing, and there is the bustle
of people chatting away at candlelit tables as night closes in on Avignon.

Looking out from the terrace of the *Palais des Papes*, the wide sweep-
ing river on one side, and on the other side the town: pink tiled rooftops à la
provençale, and swallows flying across.

Writer's trail
7th April, 2002. Toulouse.

Staying in the *"Hôtel du Grand Balcon"*, near the central *Place Capitole;*
a rare find. The hotel dates back to the early 1900s, and is accordingly atmospheric: creaking floorboards, dark wooden wall panels, musty air, high ceil-
ings and an old-fashioned mechanical lift.

But what makes the hotel so special is that famed writer and pilot
Antoine de Saint Exupèry used to stay here in his pioneering days. In the
early days of the hotel's life, when three sisters ran it, air pilots used to stay
here when they were passing through Toulouse. According to the legend,
they became regulars here, and consequently a huge family of *pensionnaires*
grew. Standing in the dark hallway, if one closes one's eyes, one can almost
imagine the ambience of those bygone days of yesteryear......

23rd June, 2002. Avignon.

"Hôtel Garlande", a charming place on a quiet street just off the *Place
d'Horloge,* with warm wooden wall panels and staircases, and cosy bookshelves
and tapestry on the walls. We are staying in the attic bedroom, the same room,
apparently, where a journalist stays every year. The romantic notion of this
grips my imagination for a moment: I can imagine him sitting typing away in
the tranquillity of this quaint room with its low beamed ceiling, while the
hustle and bustle of Avignon continues outside. He, the journalist, oblivious
to it, lost in his writer's world.

Café society
16th December, 2001. Le Mans.

I'm sitting in my favourite brassiere on the *Place de la République,* at a table by the window: a prime position from which to observe.

Inside the café, a story is unfolding at every table. Some tables are occupied by a solitary man or woman staring into the never-ending depths of his or her *espresso,* whilst other tables are home to lively groups of friends laughing and debating the afternoon away. At the bar, stand a few men dressed in chic business suits, solemnly reading the day's papers as they savour a glass of red wine.

Five minutes of people watching in a café can feel like an eternity, almost as if you've entered a timeless zone. It is, without a doubt, this sense of "timelessness" which makes French cafés so compelling, that and the element of "circular time": the same scenes reoccurring faultlessly. There are always the elderly established clientele who enter and hail the proprietor, and the waitress, gliding with the grace of a true ballerina from table to table, with her smile and sing-song voice *"Bonjour Madame, que désirez-vous?".*

It is certainly not surprising that so many artists and writers have chosen the allure of café society in France as their subject, where there's a buzz and yet a paradoxical sense of ease: the enjoyment of a relaxed afternoon whiling away the hours in a brassiere....

Locomotives

Travelling from one town to another, all your worldly possessions on your back, taking each day as it comes: freedom, a sense of being transient, life's horizons becoming more and more open with every move, every new place.

4th May 2002. Paris Gare d'Est to St Valentin, Austria.

Whenever I take a long train journey, I always have the impression of being between two time zones, and more surreally still, between two worlds. It is a period of transition: a period when you are not in any particular place.

This sensation manifests itself more than ever when the train is passing silently and anonymously through towns and cities in the dead of the night. One drifts into a semi-dreamlike state, awaking with every jolt of the train: people getting on and off at odd, untimely hours.

Travelling on the night train from Paris to Austria, which took twelve hours, was a surreal journey. The first few hours I still felt on familiar territory: still surrounded by French speaking voices. But once we crossed the borders, I would awaken between drifts of sleep, to the babble of German conversation, strange and unfamiliar. And at daybreak, looking out of the window, now on Austrian soil, the climate a foreign one: different landscape, different faces. France felt like a distant land.

5ᵗʰ April 2002. Train from Valence to Montpellier.

On the slow train from Valence to Montpellier, the train took us through an ever-changing landscape: the contours of the land altering with every twist and turn of the train.

The train chugged past rolling hills and cascading vineyards, olive trees and lilac trees: the colourful *milieu* becoming visibly more "provençal" and rustic. We pass mountain ranges with small forgotten villages nestled amid the orchards and fields of golden maize and lavender where horses are ploughing the land. The terrain is becoming more and more arid as we near Montpellier, and the sense of light is brighter, more translucent somehow.

Passing through Arles and Nimes, already a feel for what the *Languedoc is*: a French Tuscany, with red roofed villas, church spires peaking above the skyline, streets clustered cosily together to provide shade in the heat of the mid-day sun.

France has a way of captivating you, of casting a spell over you so that you become totally enchanted by the way of life there. There is something very pleasurable about a country whose people prioritise the simple pleasures of life: long meals *"en famille"* (the ceremony of *aperitifs* to begin and *digestifs* to finish still not lost), thriving food markets in the towns, a love of culture and debate, and most importantly, a sense of patriotism for France which is infectious even to visitors.

For the French, life should be comfortable and leisure time should be prolonged whenever possible, for this is not, in contrast to our own, a materialistic nation. The French themselves have a certain *je ne sais quoi,* which is difficult to define: they have creative flair and such charm and vitality that it is always a joy to be around them. What's more, France boasts one of the most romantic languages in the world as its national tongue…la langue française, c'est belle, pas de question.

My love affair with France still goes on, there are so many hidden corners which I have yet to discover: so far it has been a fine romance, long may it continue. This is a country I will never tire of.

LETTER FROM UZES
Dawn Slaughter

Uzes is a small town of around 8000 in the summer season. It's buzzing with hoards of tourists attracted by its famous Saturday market, the Mediterranean cuisine, the wine, the culture and tradition of Languedoc Rousillion, the sunshine, I could go on. However, my year here is from September to May and as such I feel privileged to see Uzes, not at a time when every passer by is just another camera-clad statistic, but during the sleepiest months when every new face is acknowledged and welcomed with open-armed curiosity. I feel I'm seeing the South of France, Peter Mayle style, where the famous images of lavender covered fields and ranting Frenchmen run hand in hand with everyday life.

My academic year abroad is spent teaching English to 15 to 20 year olds at the local high school. The more unconventional methods I use the better since these are not normal English classes but cultural exchanges. Thus, I try to introduce the pupils to Britain as it is now and not Britain as it was one hundred years ago *a la* school textbook with kids named Tom and Jane still wearing blazers, knee high socks and uttering words such as "gosh" or "chaps". In return I enjoy cultural immersion. I'm living with a French family, all my friends are French and I even watch French TV now and again! Therefore, while learning the bits of the language that I have never been taught, and trying desperately (but with little success) to hide my exasperatingly un-French accent, I also get to gasp in awe at how different we still are from our cousins across the Channel. A United Europe may be upon us but that certainly hasn't affected the Uzesians. Here:

A) We don't shake hands, we kiss

B) Wine is cheaper than Evian

C) What exactly is a vegetarian anyway?

D) We enjoy two-hour lunch breaks. This is especially necessary for teachers who need time to sober after their half bottle of rouge drunk in the canteen…

E) But of course we need at least one baker and one hairdresser on every corner!

F) A strike is compulsory every second week, even if we don't know exactly what we are on strike for.

Despite (or indeed because of) all these amusing idiosyncrasies this year in France is proving to be a wonderful experience. I have been welcomed by a lovely French lady into her home as if I were one of the family. I'm learning the true French way of life while at the same time discovering new parts of my own country and culture through the eyes of others. In turn I take pride in presenting the side of Scotland, which French adolescents had never envisaged. That is to say minus Nessie, *Braveheart* and funny looking men dressed in skirts!

All in all my year as an assistant has so far been one of the most dynamic and rewarding of my life. I hope to return to St. Andrews ready for the hard slog of honours, leaving in my wake a handful of French kids speaking English with a whisper of a Scottish accent mixed amongst their dropped h's and aspirated p's.

Rétrospectif: To all those 2nd years out their planning their third year abroad, don't panic! As you can see from my rather effusive style, your year will exceed your expectations in so many ways. You become the cultural reference point for many different kids all with their quirks, some interested, some apparently indifferent to what you have to say. The key is to never stop trying to capture those kids attention who are just too "cool" to learn, it is this that lifts your year out of taking experiences from the community for yourself and giving them a memory or a piece of information that they will retain. A year abroad epitomises the side of travel that is so often neglected during a two week holiday or gap year trip, in immersing oneself in a community, becoming part of day to day life, a sense of trust is established which allows insights elusive to the passing traveller. (I became la "petite anglaise" to most of the community, clearly in deed of guidance away from her terribly British habits!) Yet, because one is constantly filled with the knowledge that there are only six,five,four… months to go, the thirst for discovery never ends, suddenly everyday becomes a day to investigate something new, asking questions and most fascinating of all finding corners and activities which don't appear in the guide books.

ANARCHY IN BARCELONA
Kevin Tierney

In this post-Genoa and post-'9-11' world in which we live, the phrase 'anti-capitalism' has become a somewhat dirty word. However, I am proud to say I have been involved. Well, almost involved. This is the story of how my girlfriend and I nearly squared up to the World Bank, and did our bit for the future of our planet.

It began as a long-anticipated trip to the Catalonian city of Barcelona. We picked Barcelona for the *Sonar Festival* – an international dance music event, hosting the likes of Jeff Mills and Ritchie Hawtin. We knew nothing of the protest before our arrival – indeed we still knew very little upon returning home.

Barcelona is an amazingly proud and vibrant city. As the capital of Catalonia, and arguably Spain's leading city, Barcelona has deservedly earned itself a reputation for culture, architecture, nightlife – and political activism. With a population exceeding three million, Barcelona is continuing to grow at a rapid pace. Even in the *Barri Gòtic,* the city's medieval heart, Barcelona seems to grow upwards as well as outwards. This burgeoning population and continuing development adds to the liveliness of the city, but can easily get to be a bit too much.

Emerging from the airport bus onto *Plaça de Catalunya* into the Saturday afternoon heat and bustle, weighed down with hangovers and rucksacks, was a bit of a nightmare. Not having booked accommodation didn't help either. Disorientated and irritable, we forced our way through the crowds in search of a hostel. There's no shortage of hostels and boarding houses in this town, but unfortunately there are also a hell of a lot of tourists and travellers. Booking in advance is definitely advisable, especially during the summer. Despite my rapidly deteriorating mood, I couldn't help but be impressed with the city, as we trudged down broad, shady, tree-lined avenues and up twisting, atmospheric Gothic streets; pin-balling our way from one fully booked hostel to another. On the verge of collapse, we formulated a plan to dump our bags at the train station ('they *must* have lockers!'), head to the Sonar Festival and pull an all-nighter. We were on holiday after all, and we could worry about accommodation tomorrow.

I don't know if it was the rucksacks, or perhaps our just-arrived paleness, but our plight must have been obvious. In the city for a matter of hours, and already we were confronted with the friendly helpfulness of its inhabitants: halfway to the station we were stopped by a smart, amiable man, offering a room in his nearby hostel. Call me naïve, but I reckon this guy *was* genuinely friendly. Too tired for suspicion, we followed him to the bright, clean and friendly hostel that would become our home for the next few weeks.

No signs of anarchy, you might be thinking. We didn't notice it either, as we danced till dawn at the Sonar and got hugely lost in an industrial estate type area at some unhealthy hour of the morning. No sign, either, at Montserrat - the picturesque, hermit-riddled, mountain-sized termite mound, to the northwest of the city. No sign on the busy, vibrant, tree lined *Ramblas*, running from the heart of the city to the newly developed waterfront; with its tourist stalls, inhumane pet shops, and street performers ranging from the inspired to the desperate. Perhaps there *was* a hint of anarchy in the weird, semi-organic, vaguely hallucinatory architecture of Antoni Gaudí – the city's modernista darling – littering the more affluent *Eixample* district.

In the labyrinthine *Barri Gòtic*, particularly in the *Plaça George Orwell*, there were dread-locked and skin-headed hippie travellers of all nationalities, complete with dogs on strings and a multitude of circus skills. But we assumed this was normal. We spent a lot of time in this triangular square. During the day, its tall ramshackle buildings provided shade; its bar was reasonably priced and had a bit of character about it; the hippies were entertaining and its few shops and occasional bric-a-brac market were a refreshing break from the soulless designer outlets and global chain stores common in other areas of the city. At night the square is mobbed with locals, hippies, tramps, beggars and a few travellers. Paranoid tourists hurry past, avoiding the mopeds, firecrackers, dogs and spontaneous games of football. We'd been warned about this place before leaving – it's allegedly not safe for tourists – so maybe you shouldn't visit it on the strength of my recommendation. I'll admit it was a wee bit intimidating initially, but grab a seat in the shade, order some *cervesas*, sit back and soak in the atmosphere.

It was here that we first found out about the protest. Posters began appearing sporting the anarchist 'A' and a Catalan phrase resembling 'death to the state'. The poster urged people to meet at *Plaça De La Universitat* the following Sunday. We lived just down the road from this square and were intrigued by the poster. They spread around town, and a few days later other posters appeared with phrases like "Contra la Globalización", "Revolución social anarquista", "capitalismo" and other similarly 'right-on' slogans. Now, I don't speak Catalan, but I knew I liked the gist of these posters. There were also various references to the Banco Mundial (World Bank), the International

Monetary Fund (IMF), and organisations such as CNT.

By the time that Sunday came round, we'd slipped comfortably into our own version of the siesta lifestyle: instead of getting up before lunch, only to go to bed again, we just got up in the afternoon. That day, our morning lie-in had been interrupted by the incessant thwack of helicopters overhead. To my half-asleep, hangover-clouded head, the heat, white walls, foreign sounds and constant helicopter noise was very *Apocalypse Now*. A ceiling fan would have completed my flashback to the 'Nam perfectly! When my girlfriend came back with breakfast she commented on the police vans in the street outside. The poster we had seen said to meet at 4pm, and it was only early afternoon. I only really expected a few students, activists and hippies to show up and didn't make the connection between the helicopter, vans and upcoming meeting. It's fair to say I was surprised by what was happening outside and would probably have gotten up earlier if I'd realized the magnitude of the activity surrounding me.

Leaving the hostel and turning towards *Plaça de Catalunya*, the streets were lined with blue *Policía* vans. Outside *Top Shop* a gang of black jumpsuited, tear-gas wielding riot police confronted a group of shouting Spaniards. The sinister, wasp-like helicopter continued to buzz overhead. Jeers and whistles filled the air. It was hot – over 30° - and tension was high. Groups of tourists hurried in the opposite direction. Occasionally, bare-chested youths – with bright bandanas covering their faces - shoved through the confusion, fleeing some unseen pursuer. We hurried back to the room, picked up a camera and notepad and headed back into the confusion.

It's hard to say what I was feeling: anxiety, excitement, both? Tables and chairs were sprawled over the ground outside cafes. Fast food giants cowered behind steel shutters. In the streets around the square, groups of locals and tourists stood looking confused, or hurried in random directions. Riot police milled in irritable groups of 10 or 12, forming double lines. All were wearing crash helmets, the front lines hidden behind reinforced Perspex shields, the second line menacingly wielding clubs and rifles adapted to fire tear gas grenades. Most were wearing ridiculous 'Top Gun' style Ray Bans and frankly looked as confused as everybody else. Have you ever been within a few feet of a line of riot police? It's an intimidating and provoking sight; believe me. It's hard to describe the feeling those sinister defenders of the law produced in me. Are you familiar with the phrase 'fear and loathing'?

A lone man ranted passionately a few inches from one line of police.

I don't know what he said, but he earned a huge cheer from the crowd of onlookers. The square itself was empty. On any normal day, this square is jammed with tourists, busy locals, dealers, hustlers, tramps and performers. That day, however, everyone but the pigeons had been ejected, and even they were kept under police guard. I'd never seen the square so deserted. Innocently we tried to wander into the square but our way is immediately blocked by gruff and bored looking policemen, gesticulating menacingly with American style 'night-sticks'.

At the top of the *Ramblas*, a group of people were sitting, singing and clapping, facing a row of riot police. A cheer spreads through the crowd, as the police drew back to the vans. At least ten vans drove slowly through the crowd and disappeared. What the hell is going on, I wondered? I crossed the road, and suddenly vans appeared from nowhere. They emptied and a gang of police headed towards a group of tourists. I followed, overcome with excitement or anger – I don't know what I was thinking. Pausing to take a photograph, I failed to notice the small mustachioed policeman peeling off the back of the group and coming towards me, ranting. He pushed me towards the entrance of an underground car park, and before I knew what was happening, he belts me once across the legs with his well-worn baton. It was amazing how quickly anger and indignation can turn to genuine, gripping fear. Images of hospitals and foreign jails flashed through my mind as I realized that it was more serious than I could have imagined. I back off, and he trots after his colleagues, chasing down the obviously dangerous tourists. "F**king a***holes! What did they do wrong!" I found myself shouting before retreating back across the road. These guys were highly trained, high on adrenaline and sanctioned violence. And people speculate as to why there's trouble.

"There's no democracy in this world…" a well dressed, masked American youth shouts into a video camera, as we head back towards the Ramblas. Shaken up by the over-enthusiastic policeman, I no longer feel safe, and it's not the 'dangerous' anarchists that concern me. The police are shifty and unpredictable. Each randomly placed line of riot police looked as if it could charge without warning. There wasn't any obvious leader calling the shots and the police seem to be panicking and doing their own thing. On the *Ramblas*, the crowd was more relaxed – mainly confused or curious tourists. A group of well-dressed, middle-aged protestors holding placards confronted a posse of bemused and moody policemen.

People began milling away as the police shuffled awkwardly. We headed away from the square, and the crowd thinned. Police vans still raced up and down the street and the ever-present helicopter kept up its vigil. The place seemed quieter than normal and most shops were closed; but it was a Sunday and a national holiday. We hung round the *Barri Gòtic* for a breather. *Plaça George Orwell* was unusually quiet. About a dozen people sat in the shade of umbrellas or clustered round the weird twisted metal sculpture (reminiscent of that game where you had to guide a piece of metal round a bigger piece, with out touching the two together and setting off the buzzer). No sign of the hippies or even the ever-present street kids. We savoured a few *cervesas* in the oasis of calm before heading back into the action.

At four, we headed to *Plaça De La Universitat* - the advertised venue. On our way we passed through *Plaça de Catalunya*. Everything seemed to have calmed down and the crowds had dispersed. Even the helicopter had disappeared. The police were still keeping the pigeons in the square under their close scrutiny though, just in case! I noticed for the first time that each policeman carried a handgun strapped to his belt. The realisation that these goons were armed with guns as well as clubs, shields and tear gas did nothing for our feeling of security. This has the potential to get serious, I thought.

In *Plaça De La Universitat* everything seemed normal. A crowd of between 50 and 100 had gathered in the square. Women, men, children, pensioners and dogs sat peacefully in the sun. A few hippies passed suspiciously long cigarettes amongst themselves. Regardless of how you felt about this particular 'crime', it certainly didn't warrant the brutality about to be displayed by the boys in blue. A bit more cautious now, we took a seat at a café across the road. As we waited for our drinks, surrounded by news crews and reporters, we watched the crowd slowly grow. The lack of police presence is suspicious. What's going on? Unaware of the 35,000 protestors just up the road in the *Eixample* we assumed this meeting was what all the fuss was about.

Two loaded police vans slowly pulled up across the square. It was 4.30pm, police came and went, and the crowd slowly fattened. After the scene at *Plaça de Catalunya* this was very tame. Perhaps this was a decoy; perhaps the meeting has been cancelled. We begin toying with the idea of heading to the waterfront, to see if anyone is noising up the World Trade Centre (this is pre-'9-11', remember, so we weren't as callous as you think). Suddenly, more heavy-laden vans turned up. The doors opened, spilling bloodthirsty police onto the square. Without warning or provocation, the police charged, waving batons and firing gas canisters. Whistles, shouts and sirens pierced the air. We watched in horror as the heavily armed police waded into the unprepared and peaceful crowd. The crowd panicked and fled as it was chased down.

We tried to follow the crowd for a few minutes, but quickly lost them. As we returned to the square, a fleet of police vans had begun to leave – no doubt they were needed to 'keep the peace' elsewhere. In the far corner of the square, ambulances removed the evidence. Through the window of a paramedic's car, a young woman was clutching a bleeding head wound. A determined group of 50 to 100 people sat in the square defiantly holding banners or bleeding quietly. Everybody looked shocked, disbelieving and utterly bewildered.

Remembering that day, and looking back at the photos, I still cannot believe the senseless, unprovoked brutality displayed by the police. Even now, recalling that charge makes me surge with anger. Spain has several police forces – one of which is left over from Franco's fascist state (described as 'Franco's right hand' - imagine a Spanish Gestapo), and is still in operation today. However, these guys were from the allegedly more liberal Policía Nacional; thank God they didn't let the fascists loose on the streets! I've seen news footage of 'riots' and the characteristically heavy-handed police response on TV – Seattle, May Day, etc – and although sympathetic to the protestors I always assumed they had somehow provoked the police. After seeing it first hand I can understand the charges of police brutality. The minute before the police charged, everything had been peaceful. A minute later, people were left lying wounded, and the police had to contend with a violent chase through the streets, entirely of their own making. If that police attack had been ordered, somebody should be losing their job; if it hadn't been officially authorized, then *many* people should be losing their jobs.

That evening, the police gave up their armed vigil in *Plaça de Catalunya*, and things began to return to normal. As the sun went down, the square filled with a much more relaxed crowd, dancing to the sound of a reggae sound system mounted on a bus. With no police to be seen anywhere, a festival atmosphere blanketed the square. The helicopter continued to keep its beady eye on the crowd, though; again, just in case.

It wasn't until the following day that we realised what had happened in the city the day before. In the window of a TV shop, we watched in disbelief a news report showing thousands upon thousands of people marching through the business district. I was impressed with the few thousand people we'd seen, but just up the road, 35,000 people had successfully marched against the World Bank. I couldn't help but chuckle at the fact that we had been within 10 minutes of this protest most of the day, and had never even realised it.

On returning home, I did a wee bit of research. The demonstration had been successful, but had been marred by violence and destruction of property. The police were accused of excessive force and the violence and damage was, as usual, blamed on undercover police infiltrators. Had I not witnessed some of the violence first hand, I would have dismissed most of these claims, as most probably would. The police wouldn't attack if they weren't provoked or defending themselves, would they? Amnesty International had been called in to investigate allegations of police brutality and unlawful arrest. The man in charge of the police operation had been suspended pending investigation. The World Bank was supposed to discuss, among other 'neo-liberal' policies, the privatisation of public services. This may seem like a relatively harmless or trivial topic to have caused such a reaction, but consider the mess caused by the privatisation of the railways, post office and air traffic control in Britain. The passion and commitment of the Spanish puts the apathetic indifference of most Brits to shame. The CNT (Confederacion Nacional de Trabajo / National Confederation of Workers) who were responsible for organizing at least the part of the protest we had seen, were one of the leading opposition organisations to fascism in the 1936 civil war. I suppose one of the reasons for the militant nature of Spanish activists is that they have had a lot more to react against than we have.

Getting accidentally caught up in an anarchist protest and the brutal police reaction, not to mention narrowly missing one of the few successful protests of the anti-globalisation movement to date, made a relaxing and memorable trip to a lively and cultural city even more unforgettable. I highly recommend Barcelona to anyone, whether you like stylish, designer shopping, an easy-going café lifestyle, hectic nightlife, or passionate and committed civil disobedience. Definitely the most eye-opening holiday I've had yet.

"Travel broadens the mind"
Early 20th century proverb

"They say travel broadens the mind but first you must have a mind to broaden"
G.K.Chesterton. The Shadow of the Shark

SICILY'S INHERITANCE
Alex O'Hara

It wasn't supposed to be raining in Sicily. If I had wanted rain I would have stayed in Ireland. For a whole week it poured down ceaselessly, shrouding the little hilltop village in a never-ending veil of mist. At first I attempted, out of sheer disgust, to ignore the situation, and in my obstinacy had set out one morning to walk to a nearby village.

The route meandered past obese streams, overburdened by the recent deluges, and gawking cattle who were undoubtedly equally as puzzled as to why the grass had suddenly become so green. All in all, I could have been taking a stroll in some remote part of the Lake District; until - that is - I was halted by a strange looking creature that had begun to scream at me from the other side of the bank. I say creature in so far as the noises emitted from his aperture sounded far from human, though he had the familiar appearance of a man. Presumably, he was some sort of shepherd as he was cloaked from head to foot in a heavy green oilskin, which was kept in place by a rough piece of twine around his waist.

A faint tingling of bells could be heard from a dell hidden from view by a small hillock, from which the man quickly advanced towards me. One or two goats sauntered lazily after him. I felt for my old rusty fishing knife in my pocket that my Grandfather had given me. I was by this time some distance from the village, and surrounded on either side by mountains I was too weary to escape into. It was no use anyway, as the goats would surely get me, so I fingered the blade nervously as the figure approached.

I soon caught a glimpse of the man's face, which was as dark as an Arab's, but with the marked difference of having a long Norman nose, the purpose of which was to funnel any excess rainwater onto the oilskin. Two beady little eyes scanned me up and down with one quick glance as I was pondering the best possible method of sticking the blade into his neck should the need arise. The rain had by this time camouflaged my hair, so that he had been presumably tricked into thinking that he was confronting a brunette, grossly unaware that I was in fact a redhead. No more need be said.

The silence was short lived as the stranger began to speak (if I can call it speaking) in a language with which I was unfamiliar. It certainly wasn't Italian, as the few words I spoke awoke in him a bemused and blank expression. He did a very convincing Manuel impression - no doubt his party piece - although I was somewhat disappointed by his neglecting to say, "*Che?*" We were clearly getting nowhere. Even the international language of hand gesturing, of which the Italians are masters, failed to instil the faintest glimmer of understanding. Only a mischievous smirk graced his countenance. I considered doing my John Cleese impression from the *Ministry of Funny Walks* as an icebreaker, but then thought better of it. I had discerned that his intention was not malicious, only curious. I imagine he only wanted to know where I was going to on such a miserable day, and had, no doubt, took me to be a fellow loon who was seeking mutual consolation from the elements.

As I was anxious to get on my way, I eventually managed to break up our endearing conversation as I had noticed the goats getting particularly displeased and jealous over their master's new found friend. The encounter had unsettled me however, and I proceeded to take the wrong road up into the hills. Suffice to say that I was damned please to get back to the hilltop village, still shrouded in mist, in which I was staying.

The incident, if one can call it that, remained in my memory however as a testament to the divisions still prevalent in today's Italy.

When I first arrived in the village of Gangi in the mountainous interior, an area that still managed to preserve some of its Arab inheritance, I felt extremely self-conscious with my red hair, blue eyes, and ivory white skin. I felt at home as would a coloured man roaming the Outer Hebrides on an elephant. It was approaching Easter, and the preparations for the celebration meant that everyone was abuzz with excitement. With all its pomp and ritual, this was the most important time of the year for the village. The medieval church and the dilapidated castle nearby remained as mute reminders of a feudal past, although some would argue that little has changed.

Yet perhaps more tangible evidence of this diverse past may be gleaned from the people themselves. As I was strolling through the maze of meandering streets I met a boy with bright red hair and blue eyes. His bronzed complexion confirmed a Sicilian, so I was genuinely surprised by this unexpected treat. Out of curiosity I stopped him, and asked his name. "Mi chiamo Aldo", he replied with an expression equally bemused as had been given to me by his fellow countryman some days before. It transpired that Aldo, short for Cataldo, is quite a common Sicilian name. I paid no more attention to this until in the midst of the mosaics of the Capella Palatina in Palermo I noticed one depicting a San Cataldo. I asked the curator as to the history of this enigmatic saint still revered by many Sicilians. I learnt to my betterment that he was in fact an Irish monk called Cahil, who was believed to have come from Tipperary, and had sailed to Southern Italy in the ninth century. Now it was me who was looking slightly bemused and confused.

I saw in the red haired Aldo the living embodiment of the Norman French invaders who came here in the eleventh century, and who were a testament to the remarkable ability of the Sicilians through the ages in assimilating these cultures.

Apart from the bad weather it was at times difficult not to make bizarre comparisons with the isle Cahil had left behind some thousand years previously. For a start, I could associate how frustrated he would have been coming all this way, seeking sunshine and sunburn, only to find similar weather to which he was already well accustomed to. Much to my amusement, many of the older men in the village were clad in dull tweeds with dashingly debonair matching hats, a sight that wouldn't be out of place in the wilds of Donegal. They would recline in the evenings by the fountain in the little square, smoking and eyeing the passers by, before sipping espresso (the Arabic espresso is of a dark and heavy texture, although non-alcoholic and not as big as Guinness, yet for the sake of my argument I make the comparison nonetheless), in bars absent of any feminine features. It is still a very male dominated society where the women are expected to behave in a certain way, undoubtedly a remnant of their Islamic past.

Traditions prevail, such as those described by Carlo Levi in *Christ Stopped at Eboli*, when he mentions the black shards of cloth which were affixed above the doors of the deceased until such time as the elements weathered them away. To my mind this image embodies what he termed as a society "cut off from History and the State, eternally patient, to that land without comfort or solace... and in the presence of death." The image of mournfully black clad Mediterranean ladies is one to which we are all familiar with from the likes of the charming Dolmio advertisements and the Godfather films. While in Gangi I noticed numerous such indications of bereavement on many abodes.

Perhaps it has been the arduous way of life that explains why the majority of Sicilians are still devoutly faithful to the Church, which maintains an influential voice on the moral and social attitudes of the people. I was fortunate enough to see the splendour and jubilance of the Pasqueta, the Easter celebrations, where the whole community gathered in procession behind the Cross and statues of Virgin Mary and various Saints, weaving its way from the church down through the narrow streets. Everyone was dressed in their finest attire, fittingly co-ordinated to match the magnificence of the Sicilian Baroque church. In such an atmosphere it was easy to get a sense of the importance of the family and community to the Sicilian way of life, while realising how the significance of rituals and of iconography which characterised the Pre-Christian era have been carried on to this day.

To these people, Easter may be viewed in the human context of the ultimate victory over death, the realisation of the Catholic philosophy of hope and redemption through suffering. As befitting the occasion, the heavens dispersed the burdensome load above our heads, replacing it with the Sicilian sun that seemed to shine with a divine radiance. No longer would muck cling like plasticene from my shoes, or my hair colour be mistaken for brown instead of red. I could drink espresso outside like a real man and pretend I was enjoying it. In such a jubilant mood I set out for another of my ill-fated walks, this time being set upon by a raucous crowd of school children who led me into their little circle and forced me to drink the local Moretti beer and partake of their barbecue. Their hospitality seemed truly remarkable and I remained there for what was left of the evening.

To have made such friends as these was something that I considered special. Looking back however, I do not think it so unusual for such acts of kindness. There seems to be a strong moral code of ethics in the Sicilian psyche. Perhaps a fitting example of this is in the terminology used to describe the Mafia, which were often referred to as gli amici or gli uomini honori, never the Mafia. This stems from the early days of this organisation when it endeavoured to protect and stand up for the people against the tyranny of the powerful landlords, merely replacing it with yet another form of hegemony.

The Sicilian people are long accustomed to lordship. Their geographical position at the crossroads of the Mediterranean predestined their history, as great powers from Greece and Rome to France and Spain competed for its riches and strategic location down through the ages. Their culture and art is remarkable for its diversity and vibrancy, centuries of domination lending expression to the most beautiful pastoral poetry, drama and literature. The

Byzantine mosaics in the Capella Palatina and the cathedral of Monreale are the best examples of their type in the world, while the cathedral of Cefalu, with its blend of Norman and Arabic architecture, is a visual testament to the cultural assimilation and harmony that characterised Sicilian society in the early Middle Ages.

Sicily has a unique continuity with its past, embodied in the various festivals, traditions, folk tales, and in the mind of its people. It is this aspect which even now may be discerned in the faces of those one meets. That is the real golden honeycomb, the eternal and living treasure of Daedalus.

"Stupid cigarette smoke snakes its way, hypnotized and unaware toward non-existence, dissipation. Naughty smoke. I breathe heavily and watch, cross-eyed and greedy, as a red glow in a smooth, staggering crawl works its way toward me. All the while I'm hoping peace is found in little brown bits encased in paper. If not at least all that is gray and bad is pushed out of me through the porthole of my mouth. My tea has steeped and my bill is five euros. I've learned that four of those finance a two-by-two square occupied by me and allowed it to be mine until I call it quits. I'm renting space, I'm borrowing someone to hear me speak, I'm buying the company of the au lait. Five euros for ambiance. But it has taught me to form thoughts around strangers show-cased before me, like bubble-wrap. I've learned to enjoy these people as they make me want to follow them and share their purpose, make me forget I have way-too-expensive tea in front of me. My body is still, my eyes are alert. My imagination is alive and vivid. I'm thinking I've ceased to be an American, I've begun as part-time Parisian and I continue on as alone and lonely."
Rachel Kondo

IMPRESSION OF ISTANBUL
Caroline Watkinson

An airport, mounds of luggage and a clutch of strangers: to me it spelt *excitement*. I had won the "Thwaites Travel Scholarship" and was due to depart for Turkey with a small group of fellow travellers. We were staying in Istanbul and during our time there were to decorate a primary school and carry out environmental projects. Sitting in the departure lounge I wondered what Istanbul would be like. Impoverished? Crowded? I didn't know what to expect.

Upon arrival I was met by the family with whom I would be staying. I had been told to expect poor people and unsanitary conditions. Anticipating such privations, I had spent over half-an-hour trying to fit several toilet rolls into a shrinking suitcase. However, this family was evidently well off. I had also been told to bring token gifts as the family I was staying with might not have much. On encountering a large, well-furbished flat complete with stereo system and television sets, I soon realised that Accrington Town Hall key-rings and small bars of soap would be making the return flight. Still, it was a relief to have a proper shower, especially considering the work I would be doing in the next few weeks.

Our first project was to work in a primary school that required refurbishment. On our way the coach passed through prosperous suburban areas where teenagers wore *Calvin Klein* clothes and eager shoppers hurried through the newly built shopping centres. However we were soon into an entirely different part of Turkey, where the coach passed hut-like houses wading in a morass of litter and young scantily-clad children threw pebbles at indifferent passers-by. It was in this area that the primary school was located. It resembled an old warehouse: the type which never seem to be in use and have German Shepherd dogs tied on chains outside. There was no doubt about it: this would require much refurbishment. Unfortunately we were not exactly interior designers and our attempt at refurbishment certainly did not resemble anything found on *Changing Rooms*. Nevertheless, the finished result was at the very least bright (orange and yellow to be exact) and it did look more like a classroom.

Our second project involved environmental work: surveying trees, clearing rubbish and fixing fences. We travelled by ferry every day and it was on these trips that I was able to observe the Turkish people more closely. There appeared a certain air of nonchalance about the Turks; an aura that spoke of an isolated self-absorption. Turkish travellers seemed oblivious to the world around them, rarely speaking to anyone and virtually standing on the small children who tried to sell cigarettes and pens to the passengers. Upon leaving the ship a small child rushed up to me and started ranting at me in Turkish and making fervent gestures. I attempted to explain that I did not speak Turkish, to which the child stared and said in perfect English "that's not my problem."

Once our projects were finished I was able to travel around Turkey, taking in the history, culture and scenery. I felt there was still something left of the country that had once oozed so much power and wealth. Many of the grand mosques and palaces still stand resplendent in their glory. Lasting reminders of the power Ottoman Turkey once had provided a glimpse into a past that will never be regained. However, such grandeur is juxtaposed against abject poverty and a constant reminder of the vast economic problems plaguing contemporary Turkey. The old, the sick and the disabled crowd the streets; sitting, huddled together, outside doorways and on walkways as they beg or sell their worn-looking goods.

To me Turkey appeared a place of contrasts; in one respect so friendly (my hosts couldn't do enough to make me feel at home) and in another so indifferent. It enables a traveller to experience the splendour of mosques, such as that of Suleiman the Magnificent, whilst they are left confounded by visions of utter poverty. It left me with a need to return and experience again this country that one can never fully understand.

"I eventually realized that my home is within me, and I can take it with me wherever I go, leaving me much more free than before."
Anon

ABENTEUER BERLIN
Barbara D. Ferguson

Not a few people asked us if we were crazy. We were five teachers, planning to take a group of twenty students, ages 10 through 15, on a three-day trip to Berlin. We were based at an international school in Dresden, Germany, and the group was a mix of German, American and Finnish students. They had varying degrees of English language ability – and German language ability, for that matter – and some had never slept away from home before. It was sometimes a trial just to take these same students from the classroom to the cafeteria. What, people asked us, were we thinking?

The sky was just beginning to lighten to a pale grey as the train pulled out of Dresden. It was 07:25, Wednesday, November 10, 1999. To our amazement, everyone had arrived on time and had been bundled, with every last piece of luggage, onto our train. Once settled, the children pulled out their discmans and bags of assorted candy and set about "keeping themselves awake". We cringed at the sheer volume of candy hauled out of monstrous duffel bags, shared around and devoured by students who were already wired enough to rival a roomful of FBI informants.

The train ride was relatively uneventful, and eventually the teachers slipped away to share a small, semi-private compartment at the end of the *Grossraum* (the large, open compartment of the train where the students were seated), keeping watch by window reflection and the occasional step-out-and-glare. The first *when will we get there?* was heard an hour into the two-and-a-half-hour trip. The first *Is this our stop?* came well before we reached our destination, *der Bahnhof Zoologische Garten* – the 'Zoo Station' of U2 song fame. Once there, however, we bundled off, stowed our luggage in a keeping room and began our Berlin adventure under thick cloud and drizzling rain.

First on our itinerary was the Brandenburg Gate. Today, the day after the ten-year anniversary of the fall of the Wall, the TV crews were packing up their equipment and the concert shell was being dismantled. There was little of the party spirit left in the drifts of damp garbage and jagged champagne bottles lining the gutters. We walked between the massive sand-coloured columns of the Gate, stepping out into what was formerly West Berlin. We found ourselves in a busy intersection, and noted an anomaly in the concrete road: a winding thread of cobblestones that is the last marker of the Wall's original site. Making our way past the row of placards bearing the names of people lost in their attempts to cross the Wall, we rounded the corner to the *Reichstag* (Parliament). We were hoping for a tour of the newly renovated building, with its beautiful new glass dome, and joined the long queue of people at the entrance. After a while, we sent an emissary to the gate and discovered the wait would be at least an hour. We took photos of the outside of the building instead, and moved on.

Our next destination was the Zoo that gave "Zoo Station" its name. It's a fair size and the visitor follows paths through leafy surroundings, past the enclosures and pavilions that house a variety of animals. The elephants and the monkeys were the favourites of our students, it seemed, thus proving again that some things transcend nationality. Everything went well until it was time to leave: five children were missing from the meeting place. Three of the teachers took the students we had to the next stop, while Ed and I waited for the latecomers. Three of them arrived ten minutes later, which left two at large. There was no loudspeaker system. Ed checked the other exits while I waited with the three students, who, unconscious of the irony, complained about being forced to wait for the others.

Forty-five minutes after the appointed meeting time, the other two students strolled up and seemed surprised at the chilly reception they received. They had not wanted to run; their feet hurt; they took a path that didn't lead to the meeting place, they couldn't find a map, they hadn't thought to ask anyone. Some things cannot be taught in school.

The next appointment was the Checkpoint Charlie museum and exhibition. The building stands near the site of an original border crossing between East and West Berlin, the third of such guard points on the road through No-Man's Land. Nothing of the original checkpoint remains onsite; the infamous sign that reads "You are now leaving the American Sector" in four different languages is a copy, and stands about ten metres from the original's location. There is also no longer any trace of the Wall itself. The road is now a busy, lighted intersection, with shops, cafes, an American-style deli, and sidewalk vendors hawking cheap beads, fur hats, and Russian nesting dolls.

The Museum is a fascinating, often sobering, testament to human ingenuity. There were any number of attempts to get over, through or under the Wall, including false suitcases, empty gas tanks, or hollowed-out welding machines; tunnels, or pirated scuba gear for swimming across the water borders, etc. There were many more failed attempts, than successful ones. Ed and I and our small group were too late for the introductory lecture but arrived in time to wander through the museum. Even the oldest students (American and German alike), usually somewhat blasé about history, studied the exhibits with interest. One of the other teachers had been born in East Germany and provided some harrowing personal stories to add to the explanatory texts on the walls. The youngest of the students did not remember a time when there *was* a Wall, though he had been born not two hours away from this spot.

After a long afternoon of walking around, the students were starting to flag, and the teachers were hardly more energetic. We collected our luggage from the station and took a local S-Bahn, kind of an overland subway, to the hostel. It was a beautiful one, recently renovated like so many other buildings in the area. The children regained their energy during dinner there, and were eager to socialize in their new rooms. They ran excitedly through our wing, listening to music, leaning out the windows, and buying bottles of Coke to wash down whatever candy they hadn't eaten on the train. The teachers played cards and decided that no one was killing each other – an open door and an alert ear was supervision enough after such a busy day. Everyone was rounded up at 10pm, and lights went out at 10:30. Amazingly enough, all went quietly. Everything was serene by 11:15, so even the teachers got a good night's sleep.

The next morning, after a thorough rooms check – the teachers' rooms were well behind on the points awarded — we started out early and arrived at *Schloss* (Castle) Charlottenburg with enough time to check our coats and begin the tape-guided tour. The kids liked the idea of the tape, because they could choose which items to hear about, but the interest level waned quickly. The chill elegance and strict rules of the museum were not conducive to their kind of learning. The castle is elaborate, well preserved, and full of fascinating information, but sadly, is not exactly kid friendly.

The walk from Charlottenburg to the S-Bahn station, and onward to the Pergamon Museum of Antiquities was an extensive one, and by the time we arrived at this second Museum of the day, the children were fatigued and antsy. At first, they listened well enough to our guide, and showed some interest at the incredible artifacts recovered from the Pergamon altar in present-day Turkey. But even our energetic and engaging guide was not enough to keep them on their feet. In the second room, all twenty students crowded onto a visitor's bench – and we fidgeted on aching feet behind them – to listen, as the fragments of the "Gods and Monsters" relief were explained in detail. By the third room, as the mosaics of the Babylonian Ishtar Gate shone in brightly-coloured glory around them, the children had just enough energy to say, "hey, cool!" before collapsing onto the floor. We teachers joined them there. As the guide finished his lecture, four of the students were unmoving and visibly asleep, and truth be told, we could not be angry with them. The guide had not noticed, or was too polite to say anything; upon his departure, the students worked on activity sheets, we gently woke the sleepers, and by two o'clock we had found our way back to *Alexanderplatz* for some lunch. Two museums were more than enough for today: after lunch, the students were led to a local *Sporthalle* and had the choice of bowling or swimming for the remainder of the afternoon. It was a nice change and, not coincidentally, revived the students while guaranteeing that by the time bedtime arrived, they'd be completely exhausted.

The evening was a very quiet one indeed. We had decided over dinner that the students would have one hour to complete the work assignments they had been given, and then the socializing could continue. I was the chosen spokesperson for this plan, and the students recoiled in horror at the idea of study time. A lynch party almost formed on the spot, but the teachers would not be moved: retire to your own rooms, and work quietly for an hour. It was a very good idea, from the teachers' point of view. By the time the study hour was finished, the students had calmed down a little, and the rest of the evening went peacefully. There was little protest to lights out, and the wing settled down to sleep even earlier than it had the previous night.

In the morning, we discovered that some of our devious young creatures had crept through four of the rooms during the wee hours and toilet-papered everything in sight. From bedposts to windows, from suitcases to CD players, the two-ply streamers shone dully in the misty morning light.

There were shrieks of laughter and much pounding on doors to compare rooms, and then the accusations began. "Why is she so tired this morning? It must be because she was awake during the night!" "There's an empty TP roll in this room! It must be someone in here!" "No, that doesn't work... there's an empty one here, too!" The teachers were duly accused, the 'evidence' being that their room was not decorated. We made our own low speculations at the breakfast table, but came to no consensus; Ed admitted he wished he had thought of it first. But opening our room's curtains later, we noticed a few items of key evidence, obviously tossed out of a window on our side of the building, on the grounds below. There was only one other room on our side of the building, so we knew now who was responsible. However, in the fine tradition of *I Know What You Did Last Summer*, we decided not to say anything to the suspects... for now. Ed completed the final room check – the teachers lost dismally – and by 08:45, we all were hauling our luggage back to Zoo Station's storage room.

Our final day split our group into two: the younger students went to the *Technik Museum*, a hands-on science museum. The older students came with two other teachers and me to the National Gallery. The mist burned off quickly and revealed a gloriously sunny day as we trooped into the museum and found our tour guide. He was a young man with impeccable English who lead us on an entertaining, in-depth exploration of the exhibition's thirteen rooms. In echo of the theme of "conflict" for our trip to Berlin, this exhibition was entitled *Die Gewalt des Kunst*: 'the power/force of art'. Striking images of Nazi propaganda, war, violence, and social commentary were set in contrast with the colourful, lyrical German Expressionists and the simple geometry of the Bauhaus movement. The building itself is gorgeous enough, but the artwork completes the experience.

We headed back to the S-Bahn and met up with the rest of the group to collect our luggage. Then we headed to the platform to wait for our train – and to elicit bold, often disconcerting stares from the people around us. Friday is a poor day to travel on German trains: they are crowded with commuters, students, and soldiers. Our children were full of energy, were staggering under cumbersome bags, and were sprawled all over the platform. They were taking photos, making faces, dancing to music, and getting in the way. We teachers sat carefully on our suitcases to rest our aching feet, laughed when the girls fell in a heap posing for a photo, and wondered at the surliness of the people around us. There were few smiles from the crowd, few concessions to youth – just more evidence of something we had generally noticed in several encounters in the past three days: the city folk can be a grumpy bunch.

When we arrived back in Dresden, most of the parents were waiting on the platform, and a number of them made a point of telling at least one teacher, "Thank you for taking our child(ren) on this trip." One found oneself saying, "You're welcome. Glad to do it. It was great." Suddenly the memories of the stray complaints, of the group that was late at the Zoo, of the boy who wanted to make an issue of the "no touch" museum rule... all those memories sort of fade into shadows, when the parent stands before you with a genuine smile, puts one arm on the child's shoulders, shakes your hand, and utters the words "Thank you."

At that moment it's easier to remember the jokes at the dinner table that made one boy splutter into his drink; the group of girls who bought matching knit caps and strutted around Berlin like some kind of teenage mafia, listening to music and bursting into laughter at any little thing; the glee of the children who bought Chup-a-Chup lollipops as big as softballs; the incessant questions from the boy who was fascinated by the Checkpoint Charlie museum, and wanted to read every placard and look at every exhibit...

"You're welcome. Glad to do it. It was great." And actually, it was.

"In America there are two classes of travel-first class and with children."
Robert Benchley (American humorist)

Travel, in the younger sort, is part of education; in the elder, a part of experience. He that into a country before he hath some entrance into the language, goeth to school and not to travel. Essay of Travel. Francis Bacon.

CHASING SUN
Tara Quinn

My friend Elisa and I awoke, stiff and freezing, on the floor of the entertain-
ment room to the soft hum of voices overhead. As we sat up, rubbing our
eyes and various sore muscles we peered out at the snowy peaks of Albania
that appeared to be drifting slowly by. Except that we were the ones who
were drifting; in fact, we were entering lucky Hour Thirteen of a fifteen-hour
ferry ride from Italy to Greece.

The low voices above us turned out to be the third member of our
party, Emily, who apparently had made a new friend. Dmitrios looked to be
in his mid-20s with bleached blond hair and tattooed biceps. He also looked
to be quite intoxicated, both with Emily and more than a few drinks from the
ferry's bar and nightclub.

'You must come to Patras,' he slurred gently. Emily explained our
desire to visit Corfu Island first before moving onto mainland Greece and the
Peloponnese. He shook his head vehemently.

'No, you come and stay at my house,' he insisted. 'In Corfu, there is
nothing. In Patras, there is *everything*'.

That may be so, we reasoned, but we had an itinerary to follow. Sort
of.

We parted ways with Dmitrios after he finally fell asleep/passed out
just before we pulled into the port at Igoumenitsa. Our budget did not, unfortunately, allow for berths so we had had a long night on the floor in the
ferry's television room with no heat and every article of clothing we owned
wrapped around us. But shaky as we were, we stumbled valiantly to the
ferry dock and took a look around. Another much smaller ferry was docked
a few hundred metres away and we discussed the possibility that this was
our ride to Corfu. Amidst our chatter, a toothless old man wandered up to us
with three dogs in tow and began speaking rapidly in Greek. We shrugged
and looked at each other helplessly until finally I said 'Corfu?' and pointed to
the boat. He nodded vigorously and pointed to a ticket kiosk, chasing us
haphazardly in that direction. With that, we were on the next leg of our journey.

We arrived in Corfu somewhat more awake and enthused after writing postcards for an hour on the second ferry ride. The main drag of Corfu
town was dismal and disappointing, dotted with travel agencies and run-
down hotels. We consulted Elisa's *Lonely Planet* guide which basically told us
what we had already guessed: get out of Corfu town ASAP. Right on sched-

ule, a kindly man named George appeared and asked us if we would like to stay at the Pink Palace, the famous youth hostel on the other side of the island in Agios Gordos. We agreed and within minutes were sipping espresso (courtesy of George) in a little café overlooking the turquoise sea and awaiting our ride from a Pink Palace employee. We had arrived.

The Pink Palace was huge, grotesque and deserted. Hardly surprising since it was just a few days before Christmas but still kind of eerie in a complex boasting hundreds of rooms, a bar, swimming pool and numerous other amenities—all of which stood vacant. The price was also considerable, cleverly increased to include the oh-so-necessary heat in our cramped triple room. We paid however, enjoyed our stay, and the mandatory shot of pink ouzo that all guests must take upon arrival was a nice touch.

There were many highlights to our one night stay in Agios Gordos. The first was a spectacular afternoon of hiking we enjoyed upon our arrival. After checking in and dropping our backpacks, we wandered down to the beach to test the water and see what we could see. The beach had no shells, only thousands of tiny coloured pebbles scattered across a carpet of white Mediterranean sand like a collection of brilliant, shimmering buttons. Delighted, we skipped along the shore collecting the occasional stone that caught our eye and calling across to one another with each discovery. Finally we climbed a couple of large rocks bordering the town and beach and sat looking out over the brilliant horizon. The town was almost entirely boarded up for the off-season and we found ourselves with a sudden, blissful peace after the anxiety of travel. Rejuvenated, we headed for the far side of the beach and followed a path up through the wooded hills next to the empty little town. The path soon turned into a full-fledged hiking trail and delighted, we kept chattering and sweating our way up the steep ascent until we suddenly realised we could overlook the town and Pink Palace off in the distance when we paused at a clearing. We meandered through a lovely olive grove along a narrow dirt road and took dozens of pictures, deeming it our 'enchanted forest' of Agios Gordos. There was an air of surreal fantasy about the forest, with its oddly shaped trees and crumpled stone walls, making it easy to believe in the existence of fairies and nymphs. Indeed, at any moment we expected to see Pan galloping by with his pipe in hand.

Huffing and puffing more than the Big Bad Wolf, we proceeded through the forest and past a couple of little huts seemingly built of little more than twigs and straw that housed livestock. Finally we reached the summit of our hike and found ourselves overlooking a spectacular view: an infinite expanse of sea and sky with rocky outcrops along the shore and lines of blue blurring on the horizon. I felt like I was in the presence of a Picasso painting, *Blue Period* of course, that I just couldn't bring myself to turn away from. As we stood awestruck, rays of sun successfully broke through cloud to spotlight certain points in the water and kiss the crests of wave. As far as we were concerned, Corfu Island may not be 'everything', but it gave us more than enough to exclaim over in that golden afternoon.

Dinner that night was mystery meat and veggies in the good company of Pink Palace staff members and a new arrival—Lucas, from Emily's hometown of Ottawa. We first ate and made polite small talk before descending into cocktails at the bar and enthusiastic euchre games until the early hours of morning. Before bed we vaguely discussed our future travels but no solid plans emerged. We would leave tomorrow for cheaper accommodation and, fingers crossed, warmer temperatures; that much was clear.

The three of us shared a taxi with Lucas the following morning back into Corfu town after bidding our hosts and sleepy little town good-bye. Less than an hour later we were back on the water with Lucas in tow, taking a Minoan Lines ferry to Patras. Dmitrios, we felt, would have been proud.

The seven-hour ferry ride was better than we expected, brightened by enthusiastic travel stories from Lucas.

'When I left for Europe, I was the most lost individual you could ever meet' he said. We pondered this, the somewhat-cliché idea of discovering yourself in Europe and returning enlightened, independent and mature to your home country. Maybe it was just an overdone fantasy, but we all afforded it a small grain of truth. So we passed serenely through Western Greece, four lost individuals adrift on a ship named for a lost civilisation.

Patras was, as we expected, industrial and dirty. We wandered from the ferry port and found a nice downtown section where we ate a delicious dinner but unfortunately had to make our way back to the rougher neighbourhoods in search of the train station. Our conviction not to stay in Patras overnight was somewhat shaken when we finally reached the station and found at least fifty agitated Albanian men also intent on leaving the city. Apparently they were headed back home for Christmas and they were crowding the ticket booth, waving their passports and fighting noisily amongst themselves. Lucas and I braved the ticket chaos and were jostled to the front, assisted by the fact that they were quick to let a girl through with exaggerated gallantry. Later, while awaiting our 2am train to Olympia, we met two Spaniards also headed in our direction who spoke of a beautiful little town in the South called Monemvassia. We looked it up in Elisa's guidebook and were enchanted; it sounded perfect, with beautiful sunrises and a hilltop monastery. Our prayers for someplace warm and inviting for the holiday seemed to have been answered and as far as we were concerned, the further south the better. Unofficially we decided to spend Christmas there and with that, our journey acquired a destination.

It was another rough night, spent catching an hour of sleep here and there on the train and bus ride to Olympia. We finally arrived in the semi-dark of 6:30am and wandered the sleeping town to wait for the famed Olympian ruins to open to the public. With only the roosters for company, we roamed a few side streets and finally came upon an unlocked building—an empty hotel. The four of us climbed to the roof and watched a glorious sunrise over the mountains, one of our best experiences yet on the trip.

The serendipitous nature of our travels prevailed as I chanced upon a fellow traveller from St Andrews—Allison, from Florida—who was actually in my hall back at the University. She had been travelling on her own in Greece for a couple of weeks and was delighted to join our little party en route to Monemvassia. We all explored the ruins together and dared to venture into the cheesy as Elisa, Emily and I sprinted across the original Olympic track and coerced Lucas into taking pictures. We eventually hired a local cab driver to transport us to Kalamata, giving us a fascinating history lesson of Greece along the way. Next it was a bus to Sparta, costing us about the equivalent of a cup of coffee, and we explored the small city for a couple of hours waiting for the next bus down South. As we strolled tiredly back from a Spartan internet café, we turned to the road back to the bus station when a large truck full of oranges turned a sharp corner ahead of us, unleashing about a dozen luscious Greek oranges into the street. Hungry and exhausted, we were not feeling especially picky and gathered as many as we could carry for a lovely treat on the rest of our journey. In Greece, it appeared, anything *did* happen.

We spent our three days in Yefira—the main town opposite Monemvassia—in a lovely pension called *Petrina* in a luxurious yet inexpensive room. It became quickly apparent that one of the many advantages of travelling Greece in winter was the ready availability of cheap accommodation and lack of tourist crowds.

Throughout our Christmas stay in the Southern Peloponnese we learned and re-learned the lesson that the people you interact with have everything to do with the experience you have in a certain place. Indeed, the locals of Monemvassia and Yefira were incredibly welcoming and often spoke excellent English, even if they did repeatedly barrage us with cries of 'You have come at the wrong time of year—come back in summer!' We laughed;

but for us the timing was just right. The sun was warm enough and the rooms were cheap. We could explore the island and quaint villages while being relatively undisturbed and experience local customs and hospitality in the official 'off-season'. Furthermore, we had found the tranquillity that we had vaguely been seeking throughout our entire journey.

On the 24th, our second day in Yefira, we finally hiked up to the monastery and small island village of Monemvassia where we found the ruins of a former hilltop village at the pinnacle of the great rock. Once again our group was in awe of the natural beauty of Greece as we hugged the broken stone wall at the rock's highest point and squinted our eyes against ferocious winds to gaze out over the sea and nearby towns. Later, we celebrated Christmas Eve with many shots of ouzo and then a trip out of town to a dance club called Petra for some authentic Greek music. Christmas in Greece, it appeared, was ushered in with one hell of a party.

Reluctantly we left our little paradise on Boxing Day bolstered by cookies from the mother of our kindly host at *Petrina*. We travelled back to Sparta and up to Nafplio for another night's stay before the final leg of our journey to Athens. Nafplio felt large at first, compared to the tiny villages we had grown accustomed to, but we were quickly enchanted by its old Venetian quarter and formidable castle. There were unfortunate downfalls to Nafplio: it was here that Allison left us to continue on her own down to Cyprus and it was a sad good-bye. Elisa and I also had the frustrating experience of losing our goretex jackets off the side of the hill of 999 steps that we were climbing to reach the castle. We got over the losses, however, as travellers aim to do: quickly, and with good humour if possible. The views from the castle were definitely worth the climb and the sunset after our descent provided another irresistible photo opportunity.

Yet another cheap bus took us from Nafplio to Athens and we all rode subdued towards our final destination: our Greek adventure was coming to an end. Athens is an enormous metropolis, famed for its extensive history and sites, if not for the actual beauty of the city proper. We had a reunion with the two Spaniards from Patras in the comfortable Athens International Youth Hostel, but overall found the city overwhelming and grimy. The Acropolis *was* beautiful, if under construction, and the museums impressive, but the crowds and filthy streets were hard to bear after the beauty of our favourite little towns in the Peloponnese. Even harder to face was the fact that we had only a couple of days until our flight back to London; already we were anticipating a tough good-bye to both Greece and Lucas and our time with both.

The final day was spent lazily in our last rays of Greek sunshine.

Even in Athens, as our time left in Greece slendered down to hours, we found ourselves searching in sidewalk cafes and obscure park benches for memories to imprint on the collective consciousness we had developed over the course of two weeks. Shared experiences gradually splintered as we all prepared to break apart and take our own personal accounts and favourite tall tales with us: Emily back to Canada, Lucas on his way to Poland, Elisa and I back to Scotland. It ended as it began, a group of friends marvelling over the view as the sun went down behind distant hills. Our flight left later that night.

Greece in winter was not a holiday spent in brilliant sunshine with hordes of tourists in bathing suits on dazzling beaches. We did encounter many sites and even towns that appeared closed for the off-season and trains and ferries ran much less frequently. But it was ultimately an experience of intense natural beauty, a welcome respite into a peaceful lifestyle by genuinely warm people, and a lesson in spontaneous and random travelling with no pre-planning or booking. We grew to have faith in the unpredictable, to believe in mythological creatures and the myth of finding oneself in travel, to treasure sunsets with friends. Elisa and I had originally imagined our trip on the vague pretense of being 'someplace warm' for Christmas and, granted, while we were in Greece they were experiencing the coldest temperatures in decades but we were far from disappointed. We all left Greece and went our separate ways, and yet we all managed to stay connected in some manner existing beyond mere geography.

"It is music for exile, for the preparations, the significations of departure, for the symptoms of migration. It is the languishing music of picking through your belongings and deciding what to take. It is the two a.m. music of smelling and caressing books none of which you can carry—books you leave behind with friends who say they'll always be here when you want them when you need them…You stare at what your life is reduced to— all the things you can stick into a sack. It will be cold, you will need boots, you don't own boots except these rubber ones—will they do? You pack them, you pack a letter from a friend so you will not feel too alone.

"Music for cold nights under incomprehensible stars, for cups of coffee and cigarette smoke, for a long walk by the river where you might be alone or you might meet someone. It is music for encounters in shabby stairways, the music of lovemaking in a narrow bed, the tenderness, the caress, the pull of strong arms and legs.

"Music for your invisibility.

"Music for a day in the fall when you buy a new coat and think perhaps you will live here for the rest of your life, perhaps it will be possible, you have changed so much, would they recognize you? would you recognize your country? would you recognize yourself?"

'Fronteras Americanas' by Guillermo Verdecchia

PARIS, MON AMOUR
Jan Magee

An ongoing love affair, fuelled by séjours, Paris never fails to court me. The loyal lover effortlessly manages to seduce me, disarming me with her vast range of flirting facets: the sensitive, captured through moments of solitude stolen by those enjoying *l'île-St-Louis*; the reflective, embodied by those with an insatiable appetite for literary fellowship, found in the arms of the word heaven that is bookshop 'Shakespeare and Co'; the refined exclusivity of such places as *Place Vendôme* (ugly plebes stay away!); the lively fun nature of colourful *Châtelet*; the elegant *Champs-Elysées* which confronts you by the magnitude of its presence, commanding your respect and attention. These are mere tasters of the different personalities she has on offer, all united by that truly Parisien *je ne sais quoi*. So, what is this spell she casts, and what happens when the enchanted seeks the essence of her secret? This is what can happen to you on an ordinary spring afternoon in the Latin Quarter when you believe in the magic that is Paris.

As the rhythm of Paris imposes itself upon you, a walk along the Seine at l'île-St-Louis becomes more than a pleasant stroll. On this afternoon I start to feel the eyes of history boring into me, reminding me of my insignificance. How many people had lived here, fought here, loved here, died here, and are remembered here. My anonymity starts to disconcert me and I seek some validation in that home to many a wanderer, 'Shakespeare and Co'. (37 rue de la Bucherie, 75005.) Nestled in between rather pretentious chi-chi Parisian cafés is this tumbledown bookshop, a real gem in the crown of literary Paris. Here one can spend an afternoon sampling the incredible range of books on offer, from a recent edition of *'The Little Prince'* to a second hand copy of Hugo's *'Les Misérables'*. Curled up on one of the makeshift sofas-come-beds sampling this little nook's delights, it is not unusual to be offered a coffee, the chance to 'come downstairs for a poetry reading,' or even a bed for the night. Among the people you find here, there is an unspoken sense of something wonderful being shared, but never mentioned for fear of breaking the spell. The timelessness and raw humanity, which fuel this unique establishment, further the mystery of this multi-dimensional city.

All that restoration of my faith in humanity has whipped up an appetite, and with the array of cuisine from many different countries on offer in the Latin Quarter it would be rude not to indulge. The Greek sandwiches, kebab meat seasoned with mint yoghurt and salad wrapped in a pitta bread and served with *frites* are definitely not to be missed. Walking through the narrow, winding streets in search of the perfect Greek sandwich, I realise the earthiness and confidence that Paris instils in those she holds dear. The flamboyant gestures of the restauranteurs, the animated conversations between shopkeepers perched on the step of their little empires, display a certain lack of self-consciousness. This seems a truly liberated city where self-expression triumphs over inhibition. As a quarter heavily influenced by the presence of France's elite academic institutions (the *Lycée Henri IV* and *La Sorbonne* among others,) the absence of restriction unlocks the boundaries of convention, granting sharp intellects the arena to pioneer the way in their specific discipline, and it is in this 'anything goes' environment that real magic occurs.

So, this afternoon spent sampling the delights of a small corner of Paris has revealed to me a little of the mystery of her attraction. If you flatter her with attention she will reveal a measure of her true self. The Latin Quarter, as a mecca for artists and intellectuals, appeals to the bohemian lifestyle. This open defiance of restriction, coupled with real confidence creates an alternative *modes de vie*, thereby intensifying that mysterious spell Paris casts. Maybe therein lies the magical secret and seduction of Paris: the ability to preserve and cultivate her distinctive and innate *je ne sais quoi*, while validating those that challenge her. Whatever her secret, Paris bestows her charm upon you, making you feel an integral part of her mystery, reason enough to loose yourself in her arms.

"By hook or by crook, I hope that you will possess yourselves of money enough to travel and to idle, to contemplate the future or the past of the world, to dream over books and loiter at street corners, and let the line of thought dip deep into the stream."
Virginia Woolf, *A Room of One's Own*

NULLABOR BOY
William Beavington

No trees
in the Nullabor.

From steaming soil to
metallic steps

we breathed between
Perth and Adelaide. Across
a limestone plain.

we made this
epic trip in two days

and three nights
on the
Indian Pacific Railway.

For a time we passed by
space,

    Nothing,

it seemed
but vast amounts of blue

and heat.

For a time
I could have been anywhere

and nowhere.

Nothing on the left, nothing on the right
then Cook,

a ghost town
scattered with saltbush.

One sign read:
"No food or drink for 862km"

and I didn't even see a kangaroo.

DISCOVERING ST ANDREWS
Elizabeth Kalfsbeek

It's true. The only golf I've played is of the miniature variety. A 'club' to me is a great turkey and bacon sandwich. 'Greens' are simply vegetables my brothers won't eat. The 'ninth hole'? Perhaps the name of a bar one might stumble across on a pub-crawl. However, there is more to St Andrews than its golf course as I discovered after my second year as a student in Scotland.

For a start there is the university. My first day there was hands-down the worst of my entire life. With $700 in cash, I gave serious consideration to buying a one-way ticket back to San Francisco the minute after landing at Heathrow airport in London and this was even before losing my passport and travellers checks (which turned up later, thanks to a good Samaritan) between connecting flights to Edinburgh.

The customs official gave me a hard time because I did not have the proper paperwork for a nine-month stay. She probably only stamped my passport because I had become so hysterical. Not only were there tears and incoherence, but I was also causing a scene.

The three months following (well, eleven weeks and three days, to be exact) fared little better. My room in Andrew Melville Hall smelled, hence "Smellville," and for the life of me, it took days to figure out how to use the telephone to call home. Expecting to fly back to San Francisco as soon as mother gave in, I didn't unpack for over a week. (Unfortunately I didn't place much importance upon showering, either, which may have left some raw first impressions on fellow students).

My routine was one of going to classes, eating dinner, calling home, and sleeping. While home for Christmas break, adamant about not returning, I decided (with heavy persuasion bordering on threats), to stick it out for the rest of the year just to say I'd 'done it' before dropping out and moving home.

After finishing first semester exams two weeks later (yes, the school is evil and arranges exams to be taken *after* Christmas break) I decided, without admitting to mother, of course, that perhaps the new semester wouldn't be so bad after all.

About the same time, my boyfriend still 6,000 miles away in California, cowardly called to 'let me know' that things 'just weren't going to work out.' Excellent, I thought. That's just going to make life a whole lot easier.

After a week of pushing food around at dinner, praying for any type of accident (probably vehicular, prone as I am to jay walking), and generally wallowing in self-pity, there came an epiphany from out of nowhere: I was in Great Britain and, trite as it may sound, the world's my oyster. I'm able to make the most of an opportunity most people will never have. And the rest is history.

As 'college town' as 'college towns' get, the University of St. Andrews boasts 5,000 undergraduates in a community of 16,000, including many Americans, contrary to my expectations. I, as it turns out, am not a novelty. Though some attend for a semester or a year, others, like myself, pursue degrees.

Similar to friends attending American universities, I had to get used to all the things taken for granted in high school: laundry, food that definitely isn't Grandpa's, how to get around, making new friends. Though no language barrier exists in Scotland, several other factors took some getting used to.

Telling the time, for example. 'What time is dinner?' I would ask. 'Half six,' someone replied. Oh geez. Three? 'Uh...?' I'd timidly respond. 'That's *six thirty.*' Now, when friends back home ask what time we're meeting for a movie and I respond 'Half nine,' they have the same reaction—but then they just make fun of me for 'turning British.'

Coming from a place where pedestrians have the right of way, to where they are not valued at all, is a little uncomfortable, especially being confused on which direction traffic is coming from. Rather than meandering across the road as at home, I had to get used to being thought of as 'ten points' to any driver in a hurry, depending on how old I may look, or if I resemble a tourist. Here *the drivers* have the right of way.

Accents are sticky as well. Only now, after two years of watching *Absolutely Fabulous* re-runs or *Braveheart*, am I able to distinguish between an English accent and, say, Irish or Scottish. Friends at school are appalled; I still cannot differentiate between a Londoner or, for example, someone from Newcastle. In my defence, 'What do you study?' or 'What's that you're drinking?' sounds the same in any dialect. If British friends couldn't tell I was from the West coast while my neighbour was from the South, I suppose I would be a little aghast as well.

The alcohol factor stops eighteen-year-old college freshmen in their tracks. *Yes,* you *can* legally buy alcohol and drink in pubs without having to beg an older brother or bribe a doorman. However, the *oh-my-god-I-can-drink-and-not-be-twenty-one* novelty wears off quickly.

St. Andrews lacks a 'frat-party' culture. This is because students generally use the pub as a place to meet, have a few drinks and a bit of chat, not a place to get rip-roaring drunk (though things happen). It is easy to see how, without being pre-warned about the etiquette, we college-student Americans have given ourselves a bad name by mistaking these 'pubs' as 'bars' where we become loud, obnoxious, and drunk.

Another shocker is scouring through the club listings directory and discovering, say, the wine and cheese society, the whisky society, or even the ale appreciation society. No kidding.

On that note, the only thing stiff about the drinks over there is the price. Speaking of prices, they are. Pricey. Everything: Food, toothpaste, shoes, everything. Now being very aware of the value of a dollar, I hate to admit that when walking past banks I repeatedly compare exchange rates like mother might do on vacation.

You may be wondering where exactly classes fit in to all this. Let it be known that knowing I would never have to take math again was one of many deciding factors in attending the university, not to mention affordable tuition. There are no general education requirements, but instead you are able to choose any three subjects that interest you before focusing on a major. A liberal arts student can expect nine hours of lectures and three hours of small-group discussion per week. Students are expected to spend much of their own time preparing for lectures ahead of time, so the discussions serve as a means to tie up loose ends.

The town is safe (although I can say a little too safe when it comes to throwing a get-together since my flat was literally next door to the police station). It is well lit at night, and because everywhere is within walking distance, there is little cause for concern when it comes to drunk driving after nights at the pub.

In order to preserve the traditional atmosphere of the city, the town council won't allow big nightclubs or even a McDonald's. Fear not. Dundee, a mere twenty-minute bus ride away, has all the amenities a city has to offer. Scotland's capital, Edinburgh, is only one hour away by train. If you're really pining for city life, London is a six-hour train ride, or a one-hour plane ride away. Access to the continent is easy and generally very affordable.

Mother used to joke that had there been a university on Mars I would have attended (and in high school I whole-heartedly agreed). Scotland is certainly far enough. And to my horror, predictably she was right again: it really isn't until you leave home that you miss it.

Contrary to popular belief I *don't* think I know everything, and attending university at St. Andrews has emphasized that for me. But I am definitely enjoying what I'm learning, both in the classroom and otherwise (how else would I have known to wash whites and darks separately?). I can't imagine it any other way.

The guidebooks may tell you it's the home of golf. The students may tell you it has more pubs per square mile than anywhere else in Scotland. The tabloids may tell you Prince William is a student there. I'm here to tell you, starting out as a number one critic, that St Andrews has conclusively won me over.

"Sometimes you don't know where you've been until you're back."
Anon

THE END

117

ABOUT THE AUTHORS

Arkus, Danny Danny Arkus is privileged
to have been able to travel to sixty countries in
North America, Europe, Africa and Asia. He has seen
the peaks of the Himalayas, the desolate expanse of
the Sahara Desert, and the great cities of Europe. Danny confesses
"Travelling so widely you come to expect gaffs, but you also soon
realise that they add to the fun and spontaneity of the whole experience."

*Caselli, Irene Irene Casselli was born in Naples, Italy, and
lived in the chaos of her Mediterranean city for 18 years. She
moved to St Andrews to study International Relations and German
and is now spending a year at the University of Bonn, Germany
Variously desribed by her friend as "determined, sensitive and fun
she has an eye for humanity that is matched by abundant energy,"
she hopes for new countries, other languages and more
inspired words to write down and, possibly, share.*

Curnow, Sarah Sarah is in her final year as a Spanish and Modern History
student. During term-time, she lives near Lancaster, having previously
lived in Australia and Spain. She has a younger sister and brother.

*Davies, Kasia Kasia Davies spent her gap year
teaching in India. Her article is based on a collection of
e-mails sent to friends and relatives back home during this time.*

Ebert, Lisanne Lisanne is a part-German, part-American
student who studies Russian and International Relations at the
University. She is especially interested in international law, after having
travelled to Italy and Greece. She speaks Spanish, German and Russian.

*Gill, Sara Sara Gill is a third year student of French. She spent
last year as an English Assistant in a small market town called Mamers, situated
at the very top of the Loire region, in northwest France. During her year there, she
wrote a journal in which she recorded her thoughts and observations
on life in France and on her travels.*

Leadbitter, Vivien   Vivien is an Honours student studying
Arabic and International Relations at St Andrews. Hailing from
various parts of Scotland, the experiences that she relates took place
during a gap year between school and university. Since then she has also
travelled in the Middle East.

*Moriarty, Simon   Simon Moriarty is a 4th year
English student at St Andrews University. He will soon to graduate and head off
to Canada, Australia and then Ghana and Togo to teach English for six months.*

Mullard, Susanna   Susanna Mullard, from Oxford travelled to Ghana on
her Gap Year, and spent five months there teaching in a local school and
working in an orphanage. She is in her first year at St. Andrews studying
English, and this article was first published in her old school magazine.

*O'Hara, Alex   I am a freelance journalist currently
studying for my degree at St Andrews. I have had previous
travel features published by The Irish Times and The Connacht
Tribune, with whom I worked for a year before beginning my studies.*

Rawdon-Mogg, Alice   Alice Rawdon-Mogg is from Sussex
and is currently in her second year at St Andrews University reading
history. The three weeks long trip was organised by Tayforth University
Officer Training Corps and Alice followed it with a week's independent
travel. The organised expedition was divided into three phases: kayaking
on the Nile, trekking in Mount Elgon National Park and a well building
project with the Busoga Trust in the Jinja District.

*Beavington, William   A graduate from St Andrews university.
A published poet, William has traveled all over the world and his entry comes from
a family holiday in Australia, where they made the trip between Adelaide and
Perth on the Great Southern Railway, stopping at Cook and Kalgoorlie.*

To make contact with any of the authors, via the Travel Writers' Society,
please contact, 'writers@st-and.ac.uk'. No author's contact details will be
released without their express permission

EDITORIAL TEAM PROFILES

Elizabeth Kalfsbeek:

Elizabeth is a 3rd year English student at St Andrews from Sacramento, CA, USA. Her travel interests largely stem from a 'semester at sea' she spent travelling for three and a half months around the world. Beginning in Vancouver, Canada, Elizabeth went to Asia, India, Brazil, Cuba, South Africa and ended in Miami, Florida to cap off an extensive and rewarding journey. She has brought her wealth of travelling experiences to be a valuable member of the travel writing editorial staff and has lofty ambitions of travel through Europe in the future.

Dawn Slaughter:

Dawn is the fearless editor of the Travel Writing Anthology and is in her 4th year of study at St Andrews as a French and International Relations student. She originally comes from Ullapool in the North-West Highlands of Scotland and was fortunate to spend her 3rd year studying abroad in France, near Montpelier. Dawn has travelled through much of Europe, including Spain, the Balearic Islands and Cyprus, and aspires to visit Germany and Italy where she is planning to take a crash course in Italian and enjoy some local native dances! In addition to her travel writing skills, Dawn achieves daring new heights as a glider plane pilot and hopes to travel more soon, especially beyond Europe.

David McHutchon:

David is a 2nd year student of International Relations and Russian, and grew up in Lanarkshire in central Scotland. He is eagerly planning his 3rd year abroad in St Petersburg, Russia where he will be teaching grades eight to eleven and hopefully travelling a fair bit as well. As the president of the Travel Writer's Society, David has an active interest in globetrotting abroad and has been especially influenced by his travel experiences with his family. In particular, his visit to the Ukraine 1992 sparked an interest in Slavic studies, even if it involved a daring escapade with KGB agents!

David's stories are always varied and lively and it is clear where his travel writing inspirations appear from.

Tara Quinn:

Tara is a Junior Year Abroad student from Queen's University in Canada on the Bobby Jones Scholarship. Born and raised in 'small-town Ontario', Tara is excited to be at St Andrews and has used the opportunity to travel extensively while she is here. So far she has been all over Scotland and England, as well as visiting Spain, Greece, France and Italy and is hoping to travel Eastern Europe in the summer. Tara is excited to combine her passion for travel and creative writing and has been enthusiastically involved with both the Society and the Anthology.

Rachel Kondo:

Rachel is a Junior Semester Abroad student at St Andrews from Maui, Hawaii. She is in her final year of a Creative Writing program at university back in San Diego and excited to pursue these interests with the Anthology! Rachel has travelled extensively across North America and since her arrival to Scotland, has also spent time in London and Dublin. Fresh from her Easter travels throughout France, Rachel is eager in her resolve to experience unknown cultures during her time abroad.

Caroline Watkinson:

Caroline is in her 2nd year at St Andrews studying Ancient and Modern History. Originally from Rishton, Lancashire, she has travelled all over Europe, including Italy, France, Germany and Belgium. Caroline is particularly partial to Turkey and Cyprus due to an interest in Turkish history and those loveable Byzantines! She is also interested in places 'off the beaten path', like Papua, New Guinea, where she believes she can study cultural and religious influences relatively undisturbed by tourism.

Rupert Spiers:

After completing his undergraduate study in English Language and Literature, Rupert's interests led him to a post-graduate study in I.T. Born in New Zealand, Rupert has lived in Edinburgh all his life, although he would like to return to New Zealand sometime in the not-too-distant future. Rupert has travelled much of Europe, including Spain, France and Italy, and also spent a memorable three months in Seattle, Washington, USA working in the 'original Starbucks'.

Lydia Higham:

Lydia is in her 1st year at St Andrews studying English and French. Born in Dumbarton, near Glasgow, has travelled around Europe and has a particular soft spot for Spain. She speaks French and a bit of German and besides her language skills, she is also particularly interested in exploring the culinary delights of each country she visits, especially the exciting atmosphere of the daily markets! Lydia's future travel plans include a visit to Arizona this summer to see the Grand Canyon.

Rachel Drury:

Rachel is also in her 1st year at St Andrews with a main focus of study in Modern History. She was born and raised in Banchory, Aberdeenshire and is planning on continuing her way up through the north of Scotland this summer when she ventures to Orkney in August (just below the Shetland Isles). Her favourite places to travel so far have been the Czech Republic and Poland, and in future she would like to visit New Zealand.